Employee Identity in Indian Call Centres

Employee Identity in Indian Call Centres
The Notion of Professionalism

Ernesto Noronha
Premilla D'Cruz

Business books from SAGE
Los Angeles ▪ London ▪ New Delhi ▪ Singapore ▪ Washington DC
www.sagepublications.com

Copyright © *Ernesto Noronha and Premilla D'Cruz, 2009*

All rights reserved. No part of this book may be reproduced or utilized in any form or by any means, electronic or mechanical, including photocopying, recording or by any information storage or retrieval system, without permission in writing from the publisher.

First published in 2009 by

Response Books
Business books from SAGE
B1/I-1 Mohan Cooperative Industrial Area
Mathura Road, New Delhi 110 044, India

SAGE Publications Inc
2455 Teller Road
Thousand Oaks, California 91320, USA

SAGE Publications Ltd
1 Oliver's Yard, 55 City Road
London EC1Y 1SP, United Kingdom

SAGE Publications Asia-Pacific Pte Ltd
33 Pekin Street
#02-01 Far East Square
Singapore 048763

Published by Vivek Mehra for Response Books, typeset in 10.5/12.5 pt Baskerville MT by Star Compugraphics Private Limited, Delhi and printed at Chaman Enterprises, New Delhi.

Library of Congress Cataloging-in-Publication Data Available

ISBN: 978-81-321-0079-9 (PB)

The SAGE Team: Reema Singhal, Pranab Jyoti Sarma, Amrita Saha and Trinankur Banerjee

Contents

List of Tables vi
List of Abbreviations vii
Preface x
Acknowledgements xii

1. Call Centres as Workplaces 1
2. The Call Centre Industry in India 33
3. The Research Process 59
4. Professionalism as Lived Experience 72
5. Professionalism and the Reinvention of the Trade Union Movement 111
6. Professionalism Contested 131
7. Final Word 157

References 166
Index 179
About the Authors 185

List of Tables

2.1	Indian ITES–BPO Export Revenues	34
2.2	Indian ITES–BPO Employment Levels	43
3.1	Dimensions for Comparing Five Research Traditions in Qualitative Research	61
3.2	Location of Participants	67
3.3	Gender of Participants	67
3.4	Age of Participants (in years)	67
3.5	Marital Status of Participants	67
3.6	Educational Level of Participants	67
3.7	Monthly Salary of Participants (in Indian Rupees)	67

List of Abbreviations

ACD	Automatic Call Distribution
AHT	Average Handling Time
AIMA	All India Management Association
APESMA	Association of Professional Engineers, Scientists and Managers, Australia
BA	Bachelor of Arts
BBC	British Broadcasting Corporation
BCom	Bachelor of Commerce
BFSI	Banking, Financial Services and Insurance
BMA	Bangalore Management Association
BOSS	Burnout Stress Syndrome
BOT	Build-Operate-Transfer
BPO	Business Process Outsourcing
BS	British Standards
BSNL	Bharat Sanchar Nigam Limited
CBPOP	Centre for BPO Professionals
CEO	Chief Executive Officer
CFA	Chartered Financial Analyst
CIS	Customer Interaction Services
CITU	Centre for Indian Trade Unions
CNN	Cable News Network
COBIT	Control Objectives for Information and related Technology
COPC	Customer Operations Performance Centre
CSR	Customer Service Representative
CTC	Cost-to-Company
CTI	Computer Telephony Integration
DTA	Domestic Tariff Area
DVD	Digital Versatile Disc
EHTP	Electronic Hardware Technology Park
EOU	Export-oriented Unit

EU	European Union
F&A	Finance and Accounting
FDI	Foreign Direct Investment
FIET	The International Federation of Commercial, Clerical, Professional and Technical Employees
FTE	Full-time Employee
GBP	Great Britain Pound
HR	Human Resources
HRM	Human Resources Management
ICTs	Information and Communication Technologies
IDPAD	Indo-Dutch Programme for Alternative Development
IIM	Indian Institute of Management
IIT	Indian Institute of Technology
IJP	Internal Job Posting
ISO	International Standards Organization
IT	Information Technology
ITES	Information Technology-Enabled Services
ITPF	IT Professionals' Forum
ITSM	IT Services Management
IVR	Interactive Voice Response
JDR	Job Demands Resources
KPO	Knowledge Process Outsourcing
MBA	Master of Business Administration
MNC	Multinational Corporation
MTI	Mother Tongue Influence
NAC	NASSCOM's Assessment of Competence
NASSCOM	National Association of Software and Service Companies
NCR	National Capital Region
NRI	Non-resident Indian
NSR	National Skills Registry
OB	Organizational Behaviour
PD	Predictive Dialling
PhD	Doctor of Philosophy
RBI	Reserve Bank of India
Rs	Indian Rupee
RSI	Repetitive Strain Injury

SEI—CMM	Software Engineering Institute—Capability Maturity Model
SEZ	Special Economic Zone
SIF	Swedish Union for Technical and Clerical Employees
SLA	Service Level Agreement
SM	Shift Manager
SME	Small and Medium Enterprise
SSI	Software Solutions Integrated
STP	Software Technology Park
TC	Team Coach
TL	Team Leader
TQM	Total Quality Management
UK	United Kingdom
UNI	Union Network International
UNI–APRO	UNI–Asia Pacific Regional Office
UNITES	Union for ITES Professionals
US/USA	United States of America
USD	US Dollar
VP	Vice President
XLRI	Xavier Labour Relations Institute

Preface

This book presents an empirical inquiry, rooted in van Manen's hermeneutic phenomenology, describing the work experiences of Indian call centre agents employed in international facing call centres located in Bangalore and Mumbai. Through a holistic thematic analysis, the study identifies being professional as the core theme that captures the essence of agents' lived experience. The notion of professionalism embraced agents' identity, altering their self-concept and enhancing their self-esteem. According to agents, professionals possess superior cognitive abilities, advanced qualifications and a sense of responsibility and commitment to work. They prioritize work over personal needs and pleasure, behaving in a dignified and restrained manner and performing optimally and rationally while on the job. Professionals comply with job and organizational requirements, absorbing emergent strain. Under such circumstances, not only do agents perceive gains accruing from their job as consistent with the notion of professionalism but also transactional psychological contracts of employment as a means of discipline are similarly justified. Though resistance is displayed by some agents a few times, this is described as a temporary outlet to ease job-related strain, coexisting with professional identity—it is not an indicator of anti-work or anti-employer sentiment. Indeed, agents' professional identity precludes engagement with collectivization attempts which are seen both as inconsistent with the essential features of professionalism and as redundant in instances where employers protect employee interests.

Through agents' narratives, the context surrounding their professional identity came out vividly. Employer organizations cultivated the notion of professionalism in employees through induction training, on-going socialization, performance evaluation mechanisms and other elements of organizational design, in order to gain their compliance and commitment to the realization of the organization's agenda. That professional identity is greatly valued as a symbol of social status and upward mobility in the Indian context facilitated the process. Indeed, professional identity allowed agents to accept task and organizational demands in spite of the strain they engendered. Material artefacts and organizational processes were cited as proof of an organization's espousal of professionalism. Though, in reality, organizations did not fully deliver on their claims relating to the latter, professed commitment to employee well-being, rooted in the notion of professionalism, served organizational interests in maintaining conducive intra-organizational and extra-organizational environments that allowed business to flourish.

In the attempt to extend the theoretical generalizability of the core theme, we pursued three courses of action. First, we compared agents' notion of professionalism with academic literature from the sociology of the professions. Second, through dialogue with trade unionists and labour activists, we demonstrated how the nascent collectivist movement in the call centre industry is reinventing itself, keeping in mind agents' professional identity and its implications for organizing. Third, in-depth interviews with call centre managers from Bangalore and Mumbai pointed out discrepancies between the conceptualization of professionalism as communicated to and accepted by agents and the enactment of professionalism within the organization.

Overall, the findings of the study highlight how the inculcation and internalization of professional identity in call centre agents operates as a means of socio-ideological control, used by employer organizations to ensure organizational effectiveness and competitive advantage.

Acknowledgements

This book and the research projects that it derives from represent significant professional and personal milestones for both of us. Drawing on multiple inquiries rooted in the post-positivist tradition and experiencing prolonged engagement in the field have enriched our learning as scholars and sharpened our contribution to related substantive areas. Working together, facilitated by the convergence of our ontological and epistemological standpoints, has allowed for a deeper understanding and evolution of our sense of self, both individually and jointly.

A large part of the research covered in this book has been funded by the Indo-Dutch Programme for Alternative Development (IDPAD), and we are grateful to IDPAD's Indian and Dutch secretariats, especially Dr Sanchita Dutta, Rakesh Agrawal, Marc Verhagen and Cora Govers, for their support.

Numerous research staff contributed to this study including Niss, Viju, Ganga, Bibhu and Jagadeesh. Pandurangan Rao completed the transcription meticulously. Our secretaries, Vinodini Raveendran and Ankur Sumesra, as well as our teaching associates, Bhupinder Arora and Mukul Kumar, deserve a special mention for their assistance to us in our various professional responsibilities.

Data collection would have been impossible without the help of Sam, Amar and Sahitya of ITPF (IT Professional Forum) and N.R. Hegde, J.S.R. Prasada and Karthik Shekhar of CBPOP/UNITES (Centre for BPO Professionals/Union for ITES Professionals), and some of our former students, relatives and friends such as Vinay Chandra, K.G. Lakshminarayan, Srinivas Seshadri, Abhilash Nair, Vishal Shah, Gervis D'Souza, Sunder Albuquerque, Anette D'Cruz and her daughters Neetash and Suchita, Lyndon Alvares, Noel Duarte, Dilip Mendens, Kanav Kaul, Jaspreet Chandhok, Anthony Lobo, Vanessa D'Silva, Ninette D'Sa and her daughter Aneesha and Maurice Pinto. We also thank Mr Ameet Nivsarkar,

Vice President, National Association of Software and Service Companies (NASSCOM), for sparing time to talk to us.

Our interactions with Sugata Ghosh, Reema Singhal and Pranab Sarma of SAGE have been heart-warming.

Finally, but most significantly, our gratitude to our participants who made the time, as well as trusted us enough, to share their experiences with us, providing us with a crucial window to understand the complexities of their work lives and workplaces.

1
Call Centres as Workplaces

A call centre is a specialized office where employees (also known as agents or customer service representatives [CSRs] and referred to as such in this book) remotely provide information, deliver services, and/or conduct sales, using some combination of integrated telephone and information technologies, typically with an aim to enhancing customer service while reducing organizational costs (McPhail, 2002: 10). Call centres epitomize many of the characteristics of service work that have come to dominate developed economies (Deery and Kinnie, 2004), providing an intangible, perishable product which is highly variable and engages the customer in its production (Korczynski, 2002). However, distinctively, call centres require their employees to be skilled at interacting directly with customers while simultaneously working with sophisticated computer-based systems that dictate the pace of their work and monitor its quality (Deery and Kinnie, 2004).

Call centre development is situated at the intersection of rapidly expanding information and communication technologies (ICTs), reengineered business processes, a changing (or changed) profile of customer needs and expectations and a prevailing culture of occupational restructuring (Houlihan, 2000). The introduction of information technologies and telecommunications advances has expanded the types of work it is possible to undertake, while reducing costs. The transformation of telephony by the development of digital exchanges, intelligent telephone networks and their integration with computer databases; falling telephony costs and the introduction of toll-free numbers; the high degree of penetration and familiarity of telephone technology; and the ability to communicate complex information by phone in real time (Richardson and Marshall, 1999), have spearheaded this process.

Another reason for the burgeoning of the call centre industry is a drive towards reducing costs and cutting staff, both of which can be accomplished by centralizing services, reducing branch offices close to the customer, and taking advantage of lower cost real estate and labour costs in locations outside main business centres (Richardson and Marshall, 1999). The centralization of service provision has enabled firms to rationalize the work process through the extensive use of ICTs thereby maximizing the use of agents' time. The standardization of service encounters with customers and the use of functionally equivalent and interchangeable service providers have also helped call centres to achieve great speed and efficiency in the delivery of their services (Gutek, 1995). This is furthered by technological developments which allow for the disentanglement of time and place for both individuals and organizations. Companies can concentrate their customer information desk in a particular country and automatically route calls from a number of countries to this centre, without customers having to know that he/she is calling long distance or internationally. As a result, companies have begun to move some of their labour intensive operations to low wage countries (Dormann and Zijlstra, 2003), sparking off the offshoring trend.

Various facets of employee experiences of working in call centres have received research attention. In the West and in Australia, numerous inquiries examining a range of substantive areas such as skills and training, career development, emotional labour, strain and well-being, control, resistance, and collectivization have been undertaken. Chapter 1 presents the findings of these studies in two broad sections, namely, work context and requirements and the impact of work on employees, thereby providing a view of call centres as workplaces. In India, where the call centre industry forms part of the Information Technology Enabled Services–Business Process Outsourcing (ITES–BPO) sector, empirical inquiries are fewer in number and limited in focus. Here, research on employee experiences largely embraces the labour process perspective, giving a broad overview of job design, work systems and work context and their impact on employees set against a backdrop of offshoring and cross-cultural issues. Chapter 2 discusses the Indian scenario.

Work Context and Requirements

While call centres could operate either as independent organizations or as departments within larger organizations that are specifically dedicated to contacting clients and customers, they fall into two broad categories, namely, inbound and outbound call centres (Dormann and Zijlstra, 2003). Inbound call centres receive incoming calls from customers and prospective customers, with the goal of providing information, services or technical support. Outbound call centres include a variety of functions, the most common of which are survey research, fund-raising, collections and telemarketing (see McPhail, 2002, for a detailed discussion).

Work Systems and Job Design

Call centres are the result of a modern rationalization process (Dormann and Zijlstra, 2003) and represent a high degree of division of labour (Grebner et al., 2003). Though this has implications for job design and work systems, it does not translate into all call centre jobs lacking variety, complexity and autonomy. While this may be true of some groups, there are other instances of tasks which embody variety, complexity and autonomy in spite of high grade division of labour. It is not surprising, therefore, that the literature on call centres distinguishes between two models, underscoring that the description of call centres as 'electronic sweatshops' (Garson, 1988), 'twentieth-century panopticons' (Fernie and Metcalf, 1998) and 'assembly lines in the head' (Taylor and Bain, 1999) is an overgeneralization and oversimplification (Dormann and Zijlstra, 2003).

The mass service/engineering model (Holman, 2003) emphasizes factory-like division of labour (Taylor and Bain, 1999; van den Broek, 2004), with jobs being characterized as dead-end, with low complexity, low control, repetition and routineness as well as low status, poor pay and few career prospects (Deery and Kinnie, 2004; Knights and McCabe, 1998; Taylor and Bain, 1999). Call centre agents are mouthpieces often following scripted dialogues and detailed instructions and enjoying little autonomy (Knights and McCabe, 1998). Tasks have been simplified, services must conform to pre-determined design specifications and the production process has been constructed to minimize labour costs (Deery and Kinnie, 2004).

In contrast, the high commitment service model (Holman, 2003) includes jobs entailing complexity and control for employees who must interpret information and use their judgement to provide individually-customized solutions to customers whose requirements are more complex and demand specialized servicing. Here, jobs provide challenge and interest and the skills of front-line workers are acknowledged and valued. In such cases, customers' requirements cannot easily be standardized and workers require flexibility and discretion in negotiating their interactions with customers (Deery and Kinnie, 2004; Frenkel et al., 1998; Leidner, 1996).

The nature of the service being provided as well as the organization's business objectives determine the model that is adopted (Batt, 2001). This, in turn, according to Batt (2000); Deery et al. (2004); Gutek (1995) and Purcell and Kinnie (2000) determines the management of the labour/human resource process, which becomes the production line in the case of the mass service/engineering model and empowerment in the case of the high commitment model (Bowen and Lawler, 1992).

Yet others argue that the aforementioned process of determination is simple, direct and linear, failing to reflect reality because most call centres seek to be simultaneously cost-efficient and customer-oriented (Korczynski, 2002). Frenkel et al. (1998) hold that the truth lies somewhere in between, with elements of both views coexisting. In their view, the management has to adopt a form of organization which reconciles the two conflicting principles, that is, standardization of processes and products aimed at lowering unit costs through scale and transaction economies; and customization aimed at generating revenue by focusing on individual customer requirements (Frenkel et al., 1998). Kinnie et al. (2000), following the same perspective, reject the simplicity argument that call centres are either dark satanic mills or the home of empowered workers. They highlight the existence of a paradox of tightly controlled, heavily monitored and scripted work juxtaposed with high commitment practices (Kinnie et al., 2000). Undoubtedly, then, most call centres espouse a strong desire to achieve low customer-waiting times and to minimize call handling and wrap-up time as well as providing high quality service (Deery et al., 2004).

Korczynski (2002) maintains that these twin objectives are fundamentally contradictory. On the one hand, organizations seek to reduce costs per customer transaction by increasing the speed with which calls are processed, yet on the other hand they extol the virtues of customer service and encourage their employees to be quality-oriented. Mulholland (2002) refers to this as an attempt to combine a lean production model with a soft discourse of caring and quality. Her research, however, fails to find a genuine and sustained commitment to this language of quality. Indeed, as Herzenberg et al. (1998) show, the application of a mass engineering/service model to service provision seriously undermines the quality of the service interaction while, as Shire et al. (2002) indicate, the need to be customer-oriented imposes real limits on the degree of service standardization. What further complicates the process is the fact that attempts to deliver service according to a predetermined design and to routinize customers' behaviour may not always be possible because of the difficulties of removing all uncertainty from customer–agent interactions (Deery et al., 2004).

The tensions and contradictions of these two logics of having to be cost-efficient and customer-oriented and the attempt to reconcile and balance them have implications for organizations, employees and customers (Deery and Kinnie, 2004; Deery et al., 2004; Hutchinson et al., 2000; Korczynski, 2002). Stated simply, organizations are attempting to personalize their service while at the same time seeking to reduce the cost per transaction. Employees work towards satisfying employer demands, being guided by the performance indicators they are evaluated on while trying to find meaning in their work, reduce strain and enhance well-being. Customers are seeking to obtain services that are adapted to their needs and requirements yet at the same time are inexpensive and can be supplied efficiently. The mass customized bureaucracy model is proposed to represent this complex, hybridized reality (Frenkel et al., 1998). Here, bureaucracy is retained but has elements associated with professional or knowledge-intensive settings appropriate to the customization of products and services (Knights and McCabe, 1998). Similarly, Batt and Moynihan (2002) put forward the mass customization model where the emphasis is both on being cost-efficient and on satisfying customers.

The Role of Skills

Task performance in call centres requires employees to sit at a table in front of a computer, wearing a headset to communicate with the customer and leaving their hands free to enter data into the computer, if needed (Zapf et al., 2003). Though there is an overriding popular perception that call centre jobs are simple and routine, in reality, they entail many complex roles and skill demands (Houlihan, 2000). Rose and Wright (2005) maintain that call centre work is skilled work, though the specific skills required vary between industry sectors, nature of job being performed, and business purpose and model of the organization. Belt et al. (2000) found that financial services firms typically provided a narrow range of tasks, resulting in employee frustration at being unable to really use existing skills or develop new ones. Similarly, Stanworth (1997: 58) suggests that banks in particular are 'creating a new deskilled workforce in (call) centres, where there is no longer a need for qualifications' and workers are expected to function with as little as three weeks of training. Alternatively, agents in the computer services industry, who perform specialized technical roles, exercise the greatest range of skills as they require specialized technical expertise as well as the same kind of communication skills needed in all call centres to perform their work (Belt et al., 2000).

Dormann and Zijlstra (2003) and Frenkel et al. (1998) also underscore that jobs in call centres call for different levels of qualification ranging from people with simple skills who provide standard information (sometimes even reading from prescribed scripts) to frequently asked questions to highly qualified personnel who deal with unique complex problems.

Belt et al. (2000) take the argument further, holding that even in instances where call centre agents are performing a relatively narrow range of tasks, they work 'extensively and intensively' on the telephone. Many agents, supervisors and managers included in their study were keen to emphasize that call centre work was skilled. Despite the repetitive and standardized nature of much of their work, the majority of agents emphasized that certain sets of skills and competencies were required in call centre work. In particular, they stressed the expertise involved in handling customers professionally yet also efficiently and under strict time pressures. Related to this, agents highlighted the skill involved in conveying the right image to the public over the telephone. In addition, agents underscored the elements of discretion and responsibility involved in their work (Belt et al., 2000). Similarly, with regard to computer skills, though the skills called for here are generally not highly technical or specialized, but involve operating the computer, performing data entry and accessing and moving between databases, navigation provides no small challenge since agents must work under time pressure while simultaneously maintaining conversation to prevent 'dead air' with the customer and manipulating the information system (McPhail, 2002).

Skill development constitutes an important activity in call centres and hence it is a common pattern to provide relatively long introductory training periods compared to other types of clerical work. In fact, agents themselves claim that the training they received upon being hired in a call centre was longer and more thorough than what they had received for previous jobs (Belt et al., 2002). Training may consist of a range of skills, including communication and customer service skills, sales skills, product knowledge and systems orientation. The particular elements provided in the training depend on the type of call centre, the range of tasks which will be performed, and the length of training time. While information technology (IT) training is often the most limited, an orientation to organizational culture forms an important component (Buchanan and Koch-Schulte, 2000). While the duration of training varies between two to six weeks (McPhail, 2002), the attempt is to make training programmes longer and reduce turnover (Belt et al., 1999b).

The debate surrounding the skills entailed in call centre work is complicated by two factors, namely, on-the-job skill development and insider–outsider views. Belt et al. (2002: 28) state that 'the nature of work organization used in call centres acts to constrain skill development'. Agents use words like 'repetitive', 'tiring' and 'stressful' in describing working on the phones all day, comparing their jobs to assembly lines. Moreover, while they developed their 'people skills' and appreciated the training they received in this area when beginning the job, agents felt that they had not actually learned new skills while working in call centres (Belt et al., 2002). Buchanan and Koch-Schulte (2000: 54) support this view, stating that 'employees leaving call centres are not more fully prepared for other, more challenging types of employment because they are not ordinarily expected to utilize more than basic keyboarding skills, and the communication and interpersonal skills that they do acquire are undervalued'.

The insider–outsider dichotomy underscores that while there is often internal recognition within call centres of the specific skill set needed for the job, these skills are not sufficiently valued by those outside the call centre context, neither in the call centres' parent organization nor in the general public (Belt et al., 2000). Ironically, the skills that tend to be least valued outside the call centre are those which are claimed to be most critical for task performance within it (McPhail, 2002), as illustrated by Belt et al. (1999b) who found in their study of 100 European call centres that call centre managers considered communication skills and customer service skills to be the most important skills for any call centre employee. Outsider views appear to stem both from popular perceptions that such attributes are essentially natural talents rather than valuable skills and form the invisibility of such work (McPhail, 2002).

The Centrality of Emotional Labour

Task execution in call centre work necessarily involves emotional labour, performed in remote mode and cutting across specific models and tasks. During service transactions, employees are expected to smile down the telephone (Belt et al., 1999a), that is, they are expected to display emotions that comply with certain norms or standards of the organization which are designed to create a desired state of mind in the customer (Deery et al., 2002). Equally important, they have to represent their organization and its values and customer orientation to the customers, such that an indelible positive impression is left behind. Employees are expected to appear happy to serve the customer in spite of whatever private misgivings or feelings they may have (Erickson and Wharton, 1997). As Thompson et al. (2001) found, the most critical skills in call centres were not technical but social. Thus, apart from computer skills and product knowledge, capabilities such as the ability to remain calm amid pressure and the ability to maintain a friendly, positive and tactful attitude while at the same time being psychologically disengaged in instances of rude and abusive customers; as well as empathy and the ability to ascertain customer mood and requirements are greatly valued (Frenkel et al., 1998; Rose and Wright, 2005). Call centre employees are not simply expected to execute their physical tasks competently and efficiently and to display knowledge of their organization's products, procedures or practices (Deery and Kinnie, 2004), they also have to adhere to clear rules about how to interact with customers (Zapf et al., 2003), being expected to display emotions that help create a desired 'state of mind' in the customer (Deery and Kinnie, 2004), even if they have to express emotions they do not feel (such as being friendly or happy) or suppress emotions that they genuinely do feel (such as anger or frustration) at a point in time. Sensitivity requirements (Zapf et al., 1999), complicated by the absence of face-to-face interaction and visual cues, are also called into play. In other words, call centre employees are held accountable for their emotions (Hochschild, 1983) and emotional labour is used to manufacture relationships (Macdonald and Sirianni, 1996). At the same time, it is being increasingly recognized not only that emotional labour in call centres can be impaired by tightly scripted dialogues and routinized responses (Deery and Kinnie, 2004; Taylor and Bain, 1999), but also that customer participation in the service encounter brings uncertainty and complexity into the labour process. Although management may wish to standardize the behaviour of customers and limit their options, it is not always possible to achieve predictability and compliance in the service exchange. Where customers' requirements cannot easily be standardized, agents will require some degree of flexibility and discretion in negotiating their interactions with customers. This has implications for task execution, for the evaluation of agent performance, for the achievement of organization objectives, and, depending on how the situation is handled, for customer satisfaction (Deery et al., 2004).

The skills relied upon in emotional labour and customer interaction emphasize a feminine orientation of caring, passivity, communicating and making people feel good. Belt et al. (2002) quote studies to highlight that demand for female labour power in service-based economies is increasing because of this belief and that stereotypical feminine qualities are much sought after employment assets. Employers admit to recruiting women based on the assumption that they are better able to perform this kind of work: 'Call centre employers expect women to perform emotional labour over the phone, and they actively use femininity in order to secure competitive advantage' (Belt et al., 2002: 26–27). Women agents concur with this stand, indicating that they used their femininity at work, particularly when dealing with male customers (Belt et al., 2002).

Though the implications of emotional labour performance for employees across various occupations remains a contested issue, there is limited data available about the call centre setting. Lewig and Dollard's (2003) work on emotional labour in call centres confirms the pre-eminence of emotional dissonance compared to other dimensions of emotional labour (such as the display of positive emotions, display of negative emotions and demand for sensitivity) in influencing emotional exhaustion and job satisfaction. Thus emotional demands at work do not directly lead to emotional exhaustion but do so through their relationship with emotional dissonance. Emotional dissonance exacerbates emotional exhaustion at high levels of psychosocial work demands, indicating that high levels of both are risky. Lewig and Dollard (2003) found that the potential ways of alleviating emotional exhaustion and enhancing job satisfaction is to increase rewards (money, status and esteem), autonomy (skill discretion and decision authority) and support (from co-workers and supervisors) as well as to reduce psychosocial demands. Deery et al.'s (2002) research implicates the role of emotional labour and customer interaction in precipitating emotional exhaustion in call centre agents. Their work specifically pointed out to the experience of customer insensitivity and abuse, the use of scripts and the emphasis on turnaround time and quantity of calls.

Customers provide both joy and sadness to call centre employees, exemplifying Benson's (1986) claim that customers are both the friend and the enemy. While irate customers are systematic parts of social relations in service work (Deery et al., 2002; Korczynski, 2003). Korczynski (2003) shows that abuse and hostility are likely to be higher in telephonic interactions due to the absence of face-to-face contact or physical proximity and that irate customers upset agents, precipitating dejection and low morale. The manner in which agents are trained to handle irate customers is in keeping with Korczynski's (2003) observation that management knew how employees felt, but they expected them to put up with the abuse to keep business going. Thus, reacting negatively to irate customers would result in punishments for the employees. Management gives employees various mechanisms to cope with irate customers. In terms of cognitive restructuring, employees were told that they could maintain their hold over the situation by the way in which they looked at the

Call Centres as Workplaces 11

situation—they should remove themselves from the situation and not take the customer personally (Frenkel et al., 1998; Korczynski, 2003). However, Wharton (1993) cautions that this disjuncture between what employees might feel towards their customers and what they are expected to display could be difficult to resolve and could precipitate severe anxiety.

Among the other options pointed out by management, Korczynski (2003) highlights the development of communal rituals which celebrated the pleasures of customer contact, indicating that it was worth putting up with some pain in order to get some gains. In addition, management also understood the relevance of communities of coping where employees sought support from each other to deal with the strain of irate customers (Korczynski, 2003). But as Noon and Blyton (1997: 140) caution, these groups serve as a curious mixture of consent and resistance to work. By helping agents to survive the tensions of their work, these communities preserve the social order of the workplace and reduce employee turnover, facilitating management requirements. At the same time, they can develop into strong informal subcultures that provide resistance and make workplace relations difficult for management to control.

Monitoring, Surveillance and Control

Control, often euphemistically termed as coordination, which is integral to organizational functioning and effectiveness (Hatch and Cunliffe, 2006), operates via technobureaucratic and normative/cultural/socio-ideological mechanisms in call centres. The ICTs, namely the automatic call distribution (ACD) and predictive dialling (PD) systems,[1] that form the basis of call centre operations set the stage

---

[1] The ACD system automatically processes incoming telephone calls and distributes them to agents' headsets while simultaneously generating a constant stream of up to 200 sets of statistics about the activities it coordinates including call volume, duration, wrap times, wait times and abandonment rates at the call centre, the team and the individual agent levels. Not only does the ACD system set the pace of work and monitor performance, but managers and supervisors can also view these statistics, as they are generated in real time, on their desktop computers, and can track each employee's activities throughout the day. Aggregate information from the ACD can also be made available to everyone in the call centre, via displays on large electronic display boards throughout the office. Often ACD systems are connected to one or more databases using computer telephony integration (CTI) software, which allows for customer

for employee monitoring and surveillance (Houlihan, 2000). This allows for the emergence, development and application of numerous technobureaucratic measures that make it possible to control employee task performance.

While the specific parameters of monitoring and surveillance vary across different organizations, they essentially encompass quantitative monitoring which is based on the statistical information generated by the system in place including measures such as number of calls taken, call handling time, call wrap-up time, call waiting time, sales effectiveness, etc., and qualitative monitoring which is based on the supervisor's ability to listen to or record and evaluate calls, covering measures such as accuracy of information, clarity of communication, politeness, adherence to a script, etc. (McPhail, 2002).

Thanks to technology, supervisors can track the performance of any agent at any point of time. Thus, the supervisor can be aware of what the agent is doing at any moment of the working day. The computer screen also allows the supervisor to see if a call is taking more than the prescribed time. The 'time displays' adjacent to each agent's name flash at a pre-determined threshold of average call time. When an agent's box flashes, the supervisor can listen in to determine why the call is so lengthy. The supervisor can also listen in to any call, and this is done on a regular basis, to assess the agent's performance (Richardson et al., 2000: 363).

Yet, it is relevant to acknowledge that management has a choice about whether to implement any or all of the monitoring capacity of the ICTs. In other words, the ability to monitor calls does not necessarily translate into the practice of monitoring (Lankshear and Mason, 2001).

---

records to appear on the agent's screen at the same time that the call comes through on the headset. In addition, some ACD systems also incorporate interactive voice response (IVR) technology that may be used to obtain preliminary customer information before a call is connected to an agent (Adapted from McPhail, 2002). Predictive dialling (PD) technology is used in outbound call centres to telephone large pre-programmed lists of customers. Predictive dialling involves programming a database of customers into a computer which then 'telephones' them, via multiple-dialling, in a pre-determined order. It is generally used in conjunction with an ACD system which, when a potential customer answers a call, automatically transfers it to an agent. If the centre also has CTI, the customer's details will simultaneously appear on the agent's screen. If a number is engaged or rings a certain number of times without answer, the computer moves on to the next number (Adapted from McPhail, 2002).

The choices made in relation to technology in matters of job design, monitoring and surveillance are essentially determined by the call centre's business purpose (which, in turn, decides its service model) and management ideology (McPhail, 2002). Examining the issue from the point of business purpose, those call centres which are more target-focused are the most heavily monitored while those which lean towards the service, quality-focused end of the spectrum are less likely to apply the full range of surveillance mechanisms that technology permits (Taylor and Bain, 2001). Holman (2004) and Deery et al. (2004) showed that agents who were required to demonstrate greater product knowledge and problem-solving skills with customers exerted greater control over the timing of their work and the manner and form of their interaction with customers and experienced lower levels of monitoring.

At the same time, management ideology is critical as to whether and how technology is used. As Mason et al. (2002: 10) state:

> ...the availability of a technological capacity does not mean it will necessarily be deployed... Managers may or may not be aware of the potential of technologies for monitoring, and if they are aware, they will still weigh the benefits of implementing surveillance processes against the perceived costs and benefits to the organization. Further, even in sites such as call centres where surveillance is routine, whether or not staff are disciplined or penalized for variations form the normative procedures depends on management practice and priorities.

In other words, 'technology does not in itself supervise workers. It is a tool giving data to be interpreted and used by supervisors or managers. It is their choice of how to use it that affects the nature of social interaction within the call centre' (Lankshear and Mason, 2001: 19). As Bain and Taylor (2000: 12) note, 'one should not underestimate the massive commitment of supervisory time and energy employed in the interpretation of statistics generated by the monitoring software and in implementing coaching or disciplinary measures...control is what matters most to management, not surveillance'.

Most call centres employ a combination of quantitative and qualitative measures, depending on their business purpose and management ideology (McPhail, 2002), and performance on these is utilized to determine employee rewards, promotions, disciplinary actions, training needs and so on (Richardson et al., 2000). Monitoring and surveillance thus contribute to maintaining the pace and standards of work, precipitating intensity and stress (Richardson et al., 2000).

Two viewpoints have emerged in the academic literature about the effects of monitoring, surveillance and technobureaucratic controls in call centres. On the one hand, Fernie and Metcalf (1998) have popularized the view that call centres are electronic sweatshops which exemplify Foucault's panopticon. According to them, '…the possibilities for monitoring behaviour and measuring output are amazing to behold—the "tyranny of the assembly line" is but a Sunday school picnic compared with the control that management can exercise in computer telephony' (Fernie and Metcalf, 1998: 2). In other words, controls in call centres amount to an exercise of power over virtually every aspect of employee behaviour (Fernie and Metcalf, 1998). Mulholland (1999) supports this perspective, maintaining that technological advances in workplace surveillance have permitted management to achieve 'panoptic control' over workers. In her opinion, the fact that supervisors can view real-time statistics encompassing every action and keystroke agents perform, and listen to any call without notice, creates the ultimate surveillance regime.

On the other hand, there is a group of researchers who argue against the aforementioned extreme view. Taylor and Bain (2001) reject both the simplistic and mistaken application of the electronic panopticon metaphor to the call centre in which supervisory power has been rendered perfect and employee resistance is nullified as well as the post-Foucauldian version of labour process theory which reduces the possibilities for resistance to highly individualistic and self-contained acts, where employees can seek only spaces for escape. Citing the manifold and vigorous forms of individual, quasi-collective and collective resistance that their various research inquiries have uncovered (Taylor and Bain, 2001), they warn that 'the problem with looking at the workplace from a surveillance perspective lies in a narrowness which reduces the range and complexities of management control strategies to Foucauldian notions of discipline' (Bain and Taylor, 2000: 5). They hold that it is a mistake to believe that 'because the software claims to be able to perform miracles of monitoring, then complete managerial control will inevitably result. It is a superficial view which ignores the complexities of managerial practice and the contested nature of the employment relationship. It also eliminates subjectivity' (Bain and Taylor, 2000: 16).

Other authors subscribe to this stand, highlighting that technology has only altered the dynamics of control but not perfected it. In the words of Knights and McCabe (1998: 183):

> While management is achieving increased control in one way, they are losing it in another. Management had more personal or 'direct' control before and could isolate individuals' movements, now control has shifted towards more statistical or indirect means...Thus management can pinpoint their staff's productivity in terms of idle, wrap or live time; however, statistics can be, and are being, manipulated by staff.

Reconciling these two sets of thoughts are Kinnie et al. (2000), who contend that tight control and extensive measurement of the workplace do not necessarily translate into the production of a satanic mill if human resource (HR) practices are well-designed and aligned with employee needs and customer expectations. Yet, there is little evidence of the HR policies that fulfil such a mandate (McPhail, 2002).

Research suggests that call centre employees do not harbour objections about monitoring and surveillance, accepting it as part of the job and maintaining that it is management's prerogative to exercise control over the workplace (Belt et al., 1999a; Lankshear and Mason, 2001). Moreover, statistics are seen as providing an 'objective' evaluation of performance (Callaghan and Thompson, 2001). Employee reactions to monitoring and surveillance highlighted their differential perceptions of quantitative and qualitative parameters (McPhail, 2002). Indeed, quantitative measurements were considered to be more problematic for employees not just because of their link to performance measurement but, perhaps more significantly, their role in intensifying the pace of work (McPhail, 2002). Qualitative measurements were viewed more favourably, with agents stating that they preferred their calls to be recorded or listened to because it protected them from customer complaints (Belt et al., 1999a). Other research supports this latter view, highlighting that employees see call recording as a means of protecting themselves from unreasonable customer complaints by providing a record of their interaction and giving them an opportunity to get constructive feedback on their performance (Callaghan and Thompson, 2001; Lankshear and Mason, 2001). Thus, it is the focus on the timing of calls rather than on the quality of the service provided which agents find demotivating, and not the principle of call monitoring itself (Belt et al., 1999a).

Interestingly, monitoring, surveillance and technobureaucratic controls coexist with socio-ideological/cultural/normative controls. That is, apart from tightly specified work regimes designed to secure quality service delivery (Deery and Kinnie, 2004), organizations transform employers' personalities via appropriate recruitment, induction, training and performance appraisals to ensure an internalized commitment to quality customer service (Callaghan and Thompson, 2001; Deery and Kinnie, 2004; Korczynski et al., 2000; Leidner, 1996). Korczynski et al. (2000) also point out that socio-ideological/cultural/normative controls facilitate employee acceptance of management's monitoring, surveillance and technobureaucratic controls.

Contemporaneously, customers are being enlisted by management to jointly supervise employees. Apart from customers' feedback being solicited on the quality of the service being provided, they can also lodge complaints about the service provider. The involvement of the customer as a third party in the work process not only adds complexity to the employer–employee relationship but also serves as an additional measure of control (Deery et al., 2002), with employees gaining an additional boss (Fuller and Smith, 1991).

Resistance

Instances of employee resistance add another dimension to the academic debate about the extent to which control is totalizing in call centres. Indeed, the presence of resistance highlights both the imperfections in and the complexity of the control process in call centres.

Employees find their own ways of resisting the pervasive controls employed by call centres. Sturdy and Fineman (2001) have suggested that as of now, resistance among call centre agents is most likely to be covert, individual and temporary. Resistance takes on various forms. There are agents who learn to anticipate when they will be monitored and adjust their performance accordingly, who hang onto calls after callers disconnect to get breaks, who exploit supervisory inconsistencies (Bain and Taylor, 2000) and who keep calls short to meet difficult duration and volume targets by providing partial answers or cutting customers off (Knights and McCabe, 1998). Call centre employees may also disregard the organization's scripted conversational rules. They may search for weaknesses in the organization's control systems and construct free spaces for themselves 'which provide an amnesty from normal emotional labours' (Sturdy and Fineman, 2001: 146). In addition, they may deliberately redirect calls to other agents, enter misleading activity codes into the system or simply hang up on offensive customers (Knights and McCabe, 1998). Callaghan and Thompson (2001) maintain that no system can completely deprive agents of all power over the way in which they perform their job. Even though work is organized such that agents have little autonomy, the emotional content of each service encounter is ultimately controlled by them. In their view, call centre employees are '...active agents, using their own emotional skills, tacit knowledge, humour and willingness to exit employment as means to challenge control structures and bend work norms' (Callaghan and Thompson, 2001: 16). Undoubtedly, workers are risking disciplinary action by adopting these somewhat risky methods, and are perhaps worsening the work context for themselves and their colleagues (Knights and McCabe, 1998).

Many of the techniques noted in observational studies of specific call centres are examples of ways in which agents have learned to exploit the loopholes in their particular set of information systems. Thus techniques used in one centre would not work in another—in this example, the agents had to manually disconnect calls, and had a special category of calls that were expected to take longer and had higher time limits. If such a call turned out to be short, agents could extend it without affecting their call duration statistics unduly. The effectiveness of the strategy is thus dependent on a combination of technology and task-specific performance criteria (McPhail, 2002). At the same time, it should be kept in mind that these mechanisms to circumvent control mechanisms are sometimes resorted to as means of stress reduction, although due to the risk they entail, they are simultaneously stress generating (McPhail, 2002).

Mulholland (1999) contextualizes resistance within the context of the power relations that define the labour and capital relationship. Her case study of a telecommunications call centre found that the primary opposition took the form of high rates of labour turnover, including many who chose not to begin work after completing the training, a form of resistance likely to prove costly to the employee who then has no job, and which renders possibilities for employee resistance extremely low in a climate of high unemployment. In other work, Mulholland (2002) reports that call centre agents often challenge management's discourse about care, quality and teamwork by subjecting it to derision. She quotes Collinson, stating that 'making fun of a management style is a form of resistance' (Mulholland, 2002: 299).

That creative and subversive humour represents a form of employee resistance against the totalizing systems of surveillance and control, demonstrating divergence and dissent from managerially defined norms of behaviour has been brought out by Taylor and Bain (2003a). While humour provides relief from stressful routines and makes work interesting, it goes beyond coping to provide a shared sense of self and a group identity and differentiation, indicating the presence of a distinct organizational subculture that exists in sharp conflict with managerial values and priorities, that underscores a deep distrust of management motives, and that is subversive in its effects. Specifically, Taylor and Bain's (2003a) work showed that while pure clowning was rare, being shaded into teasing and satire that were sometimes vicious in character and directed at individual supervisors or management in general, denigration of customers helped to overcome alienation from work. The efflorescence of humorous activities at a subterranean level delivers a further blow to those who liken the call centre to an electronic prison.

Bain and Taylor (2000) cite instances of collective organizing and management problems such as turnover and absenteeism as evidence of employees exerting their own control. Although strike action is rare and unionism still somewhat embryonic in call centres, employees do contest and challenge management decision-making and resist unfair treatment and unacceptable customer behaviour (Deery and Kinnie, 2004). Taylor and Bain (1999) cite evidence that collective representation in Britain is growing and that union claims for improvements in working conditions are proving effective. In their survey of 108 Scottish call centres, Taylor and Bain (1999) found that more than half of them had a trade union or staff association. They pointed to a number of financial services organizations where more than three quarters of the employees belonged to a union. There was also evidence of high levels of inter-union cooperation. Taylor and

Bain (2003a) maintain that the paucity of strike action does not mean the absence of workplace conflict and resistance. Even when conflict and resistance are not overtly manifest, oppositional attitudes and adversarialism persist and union relevance continues.

Collective resistance need not be organized through trade unions as Callaghan and Thompson (2001) show. They demonstrate how collective responses by employees help individuals cope with the pressures and tensions of call centre work. That is, how 'CSRs use the loose framework of "teams" or other collective contexts to create and reproduce the same kind of informal group dynamics and mutual support found in previous generations of industries' (Callaghan and Thompson, 2001: 33). Indeed, the engagement of humour as a means of building a workplace trade unionism in circumstances of employer hostility illustrates how subversive satire could be allied to a wider collective union organizing campaign at the workplace level. Instead of considering resistance and misbehaviour and organization as polar opposites, it is important to recognize how these can jointly be used in a creative way to challenge managerial legitimacy (Taylor and Bain, 2003a). This supports Noon and Blyton's (1997) stand cited earlier that communities of coping within call centres serve as a curious mixture of consent and resistance to work.

Taylor and Bain (2003a: 1488) succinctly capture the complexity of the situation when, drawing on labour process theory, they state that 'the social relations between capital and labour in the workplace are of "structured antagonism", although capital's requirement to generate some degree of creativity and cooperation from labour means that in response, worker resistance overlaps and coexists with accommodation, compliance and consent'.

As workplaces, then, call centres represent a duality. On one hand, they reflect modern management practices of flat structure, team working, flexibility, mentoring and support which expose open management styles and employee empowerment (Belt et al., 2000; Callaghan and Thompson, 2001). On the other hand, call centres are driven by the logic of rationalization and routinization in which the essential message is about meeting the required statistics. A culture of authoritarianism and institutionalized defensiveness results, with each level of the organization putting pressure on the level below (Houlihan, 2000). The operationalization of the latter perspective is facilitated by technology.

Though the adoption of team working is seen as central to the management strategy of call centres, in reality, team working here has a narrow meaning referring to employees working in physical proximity with other members of the team, carrying out similar tasks, with shared productivity, targets and rewards, a shared supervisor, and sometimes socializing with each other outside office hours (Belt et al., 1999a). In other words, in spite of the team structure, task execution is largely a solitary activity (Brændengen, 1999). Callaghan and Thompson (2001) maintain that instead of creating a functional division of labour, call centre teams are employed to generate an element of sociability that reduces individualism and to introduce competitive mechanisms that boost productivity. Bain and Taylor (2000) concur with the view that teamwork is a mechanism to intensify work, citing the weekly distribution of team performance ratings and their consequent implications for supervisory pressure, incentives, etc.

Tactics devised by management to give call centre employees a voice are generally not utilized to their full potential. By and large, these mechanisms which include employee meetings, team briefings, etc., operate as one way processes to communicate management views and expectations and emphasize productivity and are allocated limited time due to work-related demands (Belt et al., 1999a; Lankshear and Mason, 2001).

At the same time, it is important to recognize that managing a call centre is not easy, being complicated by a variety of factors. Kinnie et al. (1999) note that call centres often operate in quickly changing markets, with fluctuating demands and unpredictable competitor actions, ensuring that managers balance a number of different, sometimes competing, factors in determining HR strategies, including the management structure of a parent organization, if there is one, actions of competitors, labour market conditions, the nature of transactions performed in the call centre, and union presence or absence (McPhail, 2002).

Impact of Work on Employees

While organizations have benefited from call centres in terms of reducing the costs of existing functions and extending and improving customer service facilities (Bakker et al., 2003), research on employee experiences of work in call centres demonstrates considerable diversity in their findings. On one hand, there are employees who consider the work to be stressful and exhausting due to its routinized and centralized nature, while on the other hand, there is evidence that some employees find this form of service work greatly rewarding, and enjoy the social interaction and peer support that can exist in many call centres (Deery and Kinnie, 2004). As Holman (2003) points out, the experiences of employees are not clear with some enjoying call centre work and others finding it strenuous and demanding. Belt et al. (2000) and Lankshear and Mason (2001) capture the complexity of the situation by pointing out that the experience of strain coexists with reports that call centre work is enjoyable.

Stress

Job design and work systems within the call centre are reported to be the primary sources of stress not only because of the simplification, standardization and repetitiveness that they entail but also because of the loss of employee autonomy and enhanced potential for management control (Bain and Taylor, 1999; Knights and McCabe, 1998). As Knights and McCabe (1998: 172) state, though much organizational analysis and most of the call centre literature tends to conceptualize stress as an individual problem, it is actually located within 'a framework that emphasizes the interrelationships between structural relations of power and the subjective interpretations and actions of employees'.

McPhail (2002) cites literature that highlights four primary sources of stress, namely, spending the entire work day on calls, providing quality service while keeping call volume up and call time down, the intense pace of work and performance targets. These four factors are inextricably linked to each other. Call centre agents are expected to be on calls continuously, simultaneously maintaining standards, achieving targets and pleasing customers, with neither opportunity to rest between calls even to recover from difficult or abusive calls nor autonomy to handle problems that arise during the call. Indeed, the role of technology in generating such inevitable stress by rendering call centres into new and effective manifestations of the increasingly capital intensive industrialization of service sector work where the work performed is highly intensive, routine and controlled, cannot be ignored (Buchanan and Koch-Schulte, 2000; Richardson et al., 2000).

While the specific nature of targets varies between inbound and outbound call centres, meeting targets assumes greater importance in an increasingly competitive business environment, exacerbating the stress produced by the quality–quantity debate. Research demonstrates that though management talks in terms of quality, in reality, their focus is quantity (McPhail, 2002; Taylor and Bain, 2001). Deery et al. (2002) cite literature to show that the tension between management's goals of customer satisfaction and customer throughput serves as a stressor for employees. That is, while management often seeks to achieve both high customer service quality and high customer processing levels, it is output targets that invariably take precedence over service quality. Although employees are often monitored for service quality, there is normally greater pressure placed on productivity. In most telephone call centres, there are constant efforts to increase the number of calls taken per employee and reduce both customer call time and wrap-up time. These contradictory but asymmetrical pressures both create role conflict for employees and impede their ability to provide high quality service, apart from leading to emotional exhaustion.

The empirical research by Deery et al. (2002) on the antecedents and consequences of emotional exhaustion conducted in a network of telephone call centres in a large telecommunications company in Australia showed a number of job and work setting variables that had a significant effect on the emotional exhaustion of employees. Call centre agents were significantly more likely to suffer from emotional exhaustion when they believed that customers had become more abusive and demanding, when they disliked speaking in a scripted manner and when they felt that management was both focusing on the quantity of calls taken, rather than the quality of the service, and unduly pressuring employees to minimize their wrap-up time. In addition, employees who, on average, spent more time per call with customers were less likely to experience emotional exhaustion. On the other hand, when the job was seen as repetitive, when employees believed that they lacked the necessary skills to deal with the requirements of the job and when the workload was viewed as excessive, employees were significantly more likely to suffer higher levels of emotional exhaustion. Perceptions of limited promotional opportunities had a similar effect.

The support and help of team members with job-related problems was associated with lower emotional exhaustion. Turning to personal variables, we see that agents who held a positive disposition towards life and work and who believed that their general physical health was good were significantly less likely to experience emotional exhaustion. By way of contrast, those agents with longer tenure were more likely to feel emotionally drained by their work.

Emotional exhaustion had a positive impact on employee withdrawal such that those employees who felt emotionally strained by their work were more likely to take a larger number of one- and two-day absences from work. The relevant factors that affected employee absence through their impact on employee emotional exhaustion were customer interaction, management focus on quality, workload, promotional opportunities and team leader (TL) support. Positive affectivity and physical health were also significant (Deery et al., 2002).

Health-related problems commonly associated with call centre work include anxiety, depression, mental fatigue, sleep disturbances, headache, eyestrain, repetitive strain injury (RSI), voice loss, auditory disorders, burnout, back problems and high blood pressure. Consequently, absenteeism and sick leave are common. Yet surprisingly, health related concerns have not been systematically researched by academics but are more focused upon by trade unions and industry regulations (McPhail, 2002). Taylor et al. (2003), who concur that health implications of call centre work have not been systematically investigated, review available literature on health issues associated with call centre employment, highlighting the role of the trade union and industrial relations movement in raising these concerns. Health problems encompass stress, voice loss (including symptoms such as pain, smarting, burning, swelling, coughs, crackling) and hearing difficulties, in addition to inadequate breaks and equipment-related issues.

The empirical study by Taylor et al. (2003) fills a gap in our knowledge. This study, conducted in a Scottish call centre over a period of 2 years, compared the health of call handlers with that of non-call handlers and linked the experience of symptoms with three aspects of the work system, namely, the social environment (work organization, job design, managerial control systems, industrial relations context), the proximate environment (work technology and workstation design) and the ambient environment (work building, lighting, temperature, air quality and acoustics). The two most frequently reported complaints were physical tiredness and mental fatigue among all respondents, though call handlers were affected to a greater extent compared to non-call handlers. Both complaints have multiple causes associated with variables relating to the social, proximate and ambient environments. While both groups experienced stress, call handlers were twice more likely to be regularly stressed than non-call handlers. The incidence of stress among call handlers points to the unique experience of call handling and its effects on health and well-being, underscoring the relevance of the social environment at work. Stiff neck, stiff shoulders, sore eyes, backaches, headaches and impaired vision followed in the list of symptoms, pointing out to the presence of musculoskeletal disorders that do not appear to be related specifically to call handling. Other symptoms experienced to a statistically significant greater degree by call handlers included sore throats, coughs and voice loss, caused by prolonged use of vocal cords in repetitive patterns, in non-supportive ambient environments. Earaches, present mainly among call handlers, appear to be directly related to problems with headsets and auditory environment. Taylor et al. (2003) further found that call centre employees experience these symptoms in clusters. Forty per cent of respondents experienced at least three symptoms either daily or several times a week while 11 per cent reported at least eight complaints. Three quarters experienced a minimum of three symptoms at least several times a month. In all cases, call handlers were disproportionately affected. While some symptoms can be individually attributed to one of the three dimensions of the work environment, the experience of symptom clusters gives a good indication of how a poor fit between the dimensions of the overall work system magnifies the experience of ill-health.

Employee withdrawal, either in a temporary or permanent form, which is a pervasive feature of call centre work, represents a means of coping with stress. For example, a nationwide survey in Britain found annual average turnover rates in 2002 of over 30 per cent (Call Centres, 2002). In the financial services sector, almost half of the centres surveyed experienced annual turnover rates of between

25 and 50 per cent and almost a fifth of outsourced operations had annual turnover in excess of 100 per cent (Call Centres, 2002). Both turnover and absenteeism can be seen as a form of exit involving an effort to escape from working conditions that are viewed as unpleasant (Deery and Kinnie, 2004).

Tricks to circumvent control mechanisms, such as those discussed in the section on resistance, are sometimes mentioned as attempts at stress reduction, although they are unreliable in this role as they may also increase stress. Others mention social interaction squeezed into brief moments. Callaghan and Thompson (2001) describe agents using humorous (or rude) gestures towards the phone or making faces at colleagues to defuse stress over angry or abusive callers and making jokes to combat the tedium of the day. Lankshear and Mason (2001) describe a similarly social approach to reducing tension in one of the sites they observed, where agents often laughed and joked with one another in intervals between calls, with management's approval. More formally, some call centres include stress management as a component in training programmes, and many have, or claim to have, team debriefings which permit staff to vent frustrations while discussing difficult calls or dissatisfactions with elements of work.

Well-being

Holman's (2004) review of literature on employee well-being in call centres underscores the importance of four factors, namely, job design, performance monitoring, HR practices and TL support. Citing earlier research, Holman (2004) highlights that where job design is concerned, control, variety and the demands placed on employees are important predictors of well-being. With regard to job control, call centres vary in the extent to which they give CSRs discretion over work tasks. High job control has been found to be positively associated with job satisfaction, while the use of scripts, which restricts what agents can say to customers, has shown a positive association with emotional exhaustion. Agents' work also has differing amounts of variety. Whereas many agents have to deal with the same type of call and have little opportunity to do other tasks, others have more varied and less monotonous work as they are able to deal with different types of calls and are able to combine their extensive product or service knowledge with their IT and customer service skills to provide a service that is tailored to meet the needs of the customer. Routinized work which involves little variety is positively associated with emotional exhaustion. Similarly, high workload demands are associated with emotional exhaustion (Holman, 2004).

Holman's (2004) review suggests that when performance monitoring in call centres is used developmentally rather than punitively, it is positively associated with well-being whereas when performance monitoring is excessive and too frequent, it has a negative association with well-being. In other words, the immediacy of feedback, the use of constructive feedback and the clarity of rating criteria were all positively related to satisfaction with the monitoring system, which in turn was related to job satisfaction. Call centre employees generally accepted electronic monitoring when they could see its place within a broader system of appraisal and development.

Research on HR practices and TL support in call centres has demonstrated that they have a positive effect on employee well-being. The perceived fairness of the payment system, the usefulness of performance appraisal, the adequacy of training and social support from TLs have all been linked to job satisfaction (Holman, 2004).

Holman's (2004) own empirical research conducted in three different call centres of a UK (United Kingdom) bank demonstrated that job control has a positive association with well-being, specifically with low anxiety and depression and high intrinsic and extrinsic job satisfaction, while job variety has a positive association with intrinsic job satisfaction. Within job control, method control had a greater effect on well-being as compared to timing control. That is, agents' control over how they talk to customers and how they complete a task is more important than their control over when a call is taken. Job demand was positively associated with both anxiety and intrinsic job satisfaction. Thus, although the requirement to pay constant attention to one's work may cause feelings of anxiety, actively attending to and meeting customer needs is simultaneously satisfying. High levels of monitoring have negative association with well-being, highlighting that excessive monitoring may have the opposite effect on performance compared to the one intended. Employees' evaluations of HR practices (namely, the fairness of the payment system, the usefulness of the performance

Call Centres as Workplaces 27

appraisal and the adequacy of training) were negatively associated with depression and positively associated with extrinsic job satisfaction. Team leader support demonstrated a high positive association with well-being.

Though there is a paucity of research examining differences in employee well-being between call centre work and other forms of work, Holman (2004) cites literature to illustrate that findings here are mixed. Some studies reveal lower satisfaction, higher emotional exhaustion and higher degree of psychosomatic complaints among call centre employees compared to employees in other jobs whereas others report no differences. Holman (2004) also compared his empirical findings with findings on well-being in other forms of work, and discovered that call centre work compares favourably with shop floor manufacturing and clerical work. While one call centre group in Holman's study had lower levels of well-being compared to clerical and shop floor employees, the other two call centre groups had both similar and higher levels of well-being than clerical and shop floor workers. These findings indicate that call centres are not radically new or different forms of work organization and the lessons learnt in other workplaces can be applied here too.

Issues relating to working time arrangements and work-life balance affect the well-being of call centre workers. Paul and Huws (2002) highlight that call centre organizations are under pressure to maximize availability and operate into the night or round the clock to meet demand or respond to customers in different time zones, with consequences for the work and personal lives of employees. A UK-based survey shows that while call centres here have the some of longest working hours in Europe with one-third operating 24 hours a day and three-fourths operating 365 days a year, very few of these offered their employees flexibility to balance their work and personal responsibilities. One-third of the organizations offered their employees a choice over shift arrangements, one-fourth provided flexitime and 20 per cent had a choice about starting and finishing times. These practices continued even though the respondent organizations recognized that improvements in work-life balance would improve staff retention, minimize absenteeism and reduce stress (Call Centres, 2002).

Hyman et al. (2003) also demonstrate that for call centre agents, work intrudes into their private space through exhaustion, sleeplessness and its conscious omnipresence. Culture management has been used effectively to manipulate and blur the traditional boundaries that have typically divided work life and private life as a method of extending organizational control. There is a purposeful attempt to manipulate and control the boundaries between the inside and outside spaces of employment in a way which brings the outside space of consumption, leisure and spiritual development onto the site of production, and pushing the inside sphere of corporate culture out into other aspects of employees' lives (Spicer and Fleming, 2004). This is often managed through emphasis on team structures that encourage and intensify self-control as attendance and active participation in team meetings and recreational events determine pay increase and promotions (van den Broek, 2004).

Studies examining the coexistence of stress and well-being, and their related variables such as emotional exhaustion and job satisfaction, in the call centre context have also been conducted. Deery et al. (2004) studied employee well-being and employee exhaustion in two Australian call centres which had differing models. Flightco operated on the high commitment, empowerment and high involvement approach whereas Telco operated on the mass engineering, production line and mass service approach. CSRs at Flightco were more satisfied and less emotionally exhausted as compared to those at Telco. Though both groups indicated that they had to work very hard, Flightco employees had more autonomy and less emphasis on speed, with a more congenial work environment that embodied employee respect and encouragement, supervisory support and social interaction. Flightco provided better training, higher distributive justice and more promotional opportunities. Employee job satisfaction was positively related to promotional opportunities, skill use, distributive justice, supervisory support, social interaction and autonomy and training but was negatively related to employee exhaustion, perceptions of high work load and management pressure to reduce wrap-up time. Employee exhaustion was positively associated with high workloads and pressure to reduce wrap-up time while being negatively associated with promotional opportunities, distributive justice, training, supervisory support, skill use, autonomy and social interaction. Overall, job satisfaction was associated with significantly lower levels of employee exhaustion.

Grebner et al. (2003) compared call centre agents with workers in traditional occupations such as cooks, bank clerks, nurses, sales assistants and electronic technicians who had undergone long-term vocational training, on variables pertaining to employee strain and well-being. While the call centre agents had lower job control, job variety and job complexity as compared to those in traditional jobs, the latter group showed higher task-related stress. Both the groups had comparable organization problems and social stressors. Though call centre agents reported higher psychosomatic complaints and resigned attitudes towards work, but were lower on irritation and strain, both groups had comparable levels of job satisfaction and affective commitment, though call centre agents reported lower intention to quit.

Task-related stressors, social stressors and emotional dissonance were positively related to psychosomatic complaints, irritated reactions, inability to switch off, resigned attitude towards the job and intention to quit but were negatively associated with job satisfaction and affective commitment. Both task-related and social stressors predict well-being. Also, it is important to note that the social stressors being referred to here are intra-organizational ones, not customer-related factors. That emotional dissonance explained variance over and above other investigated task and social stressors adds further evidence to the role of employee work in service organizations and underscores the role of employee dissonance as a stressor in its own right (Grebner et al., 2003).

Job control was positively related to job satisfaction and affective commitment and negatively associated with irritated reactions, psychosomatic complaints, resigned attitudes towards the job and intention to quit. Job complexity was positively associated with job satisfaction and affective commitment but had a negative association with intention to quit. Organizations therefore need to consider ways of increasing job control and job complexity. Additionally, they need to consider ways to handle social stressors and integrate them into stress-related job analysis, suggesting that social stressors should receive more attention than they have so far (Grebner et al., 2003).

The cross-national studies conducted by Frenkel et al. (1998; 1999) suggest quite high levels of overall job satisfaction, with nearly three-quarters of their respondents reporting that some satisfaction appears to be derived from helping customers and from the camaraderie and social support that develops in the work environment. Further, performance monitoring seemed to be fairly widely accepted, although that acceptance was contingent upon the style of supervision. Over half the respondents were satisfied or very satisfied with the methods of control used and three-quarters said that the controls helped them to work better (Frenkel et al., 1998).

The concomitance of job-related strain and well-being for employees is effectively captured by the job demands resources (JDR) model which points out the coexistence of two specific sets of working conditions, namely, job demands including physical, social or organizational aspects of the job that require sustained physical and/or psychological effort on the part of the employee and are therefore associated with strain and job resources including physical, psychological, social or organizational aspects of the job that reduce job demands, facilitate the achievement of work goals and stimulate personal growth and development, thereby leading to well-being. Jobs demands deplete energy and lead to health problems (the health impairment hypothesis) while job resources energize and lead to greater motivation, dedication and commitment (the motivational hypothesis) (Demerouti et al., 2001). Bakker et al. (2003) tested this model among 477 call centre agents working in a Dutch call centre and found empirical support for it. Accordingly, job demands were the most important predictors of health problems and hence absenteeism while job resources were the most important predictors of involvement and motivation and hence turnover intentions. Clearly, dual processes of energy depletion and motivation exist among call centre employees. The findings of Bakker et al. (2003) replicate and expand previous findings with the JDR model among other occupational groups such as air traffic controllers, human service professionals and production workers. That is, the underlying processes of energy depletion, where job demands are linked to strain, and of motivation, where job resources are linked to well-being, show similarity across a range of occupational groups, though specific demands and resources vary in different jobs.

From an employee's long-term perspective, the value of call centre work has been questioned on the grounds that it is monotonous and lacks career opportunities (McPhail, 2002). This is because the combination of Taylorist fragmentation of work and flat organizational structures restricts growth (Richardson et al., 2000). Lankshear and Mason (2001) found that the majority of agents in their study sites recognized but accepted this, adopting the instrumental attitude that it was a well-paying job rather than a career.

It is thus difficult for call centre agents to move out of this sector into another one, without furthering their qualifications and skills, unless the alternate job calls for a similar repertoire of abilities. In such instances, though, it is quite probable that the transition does not translate into a career development move or a career growth opportunity but remains another comparable job in another industry. Similarly, it is also difficult for call centre agents to move up the hierarchy beyond supervisory levels into management positions in their current organizations or in other organizations in the same sector. While this is partially because of paucity of management positions in this industry (Belt et al., 2000), the other relevant explanation is the agents' lack of appropriate qualification and skill. Only in instances where qualifications and skills are sufficiently upgraded does such horizontal movement become a possibility. Interestingly, supervisory training presents significant gaps. Belt et al. (1999a) showed that while substantial introductory training is given to new supervisors, no or limited on-the-job training is given to supervisors or TLs promoted from within the organization, making it difficult for them to learn the skills they would need to be considered for the next level of promotion (Belt et al., 2002). Further, Belt et al. (2000) point out that it is difficult for a call centre agent to move to a position elsewhere in the parent organization, if one exists. This is essentially because of the perceived low status of call centres within the parent organization.

The lack of appropriately skilled junior and middle management in call centres has been noted by Belt et al. (2002) and Houlihan (2001), who highlight that these groups not only face conflicting goals but also are expected to learn on the job, in the absence of opportunities for professional development and strategic support. Management's commitment to employee development and empowerment in call centres is thus questionable (Bain and Taylor, 1999).

At the same time, labour turnover is high (Bain and Taylor, 1999; Taylor and Bain, 1999). Researchers have pointed out that high labour turnover and absenteeism rates adversely affect the efficiency of call centres. The reasons attributed to this are the pressures of job, lack of promotion opportunities, working time, work-life balance, 'phone rage' and the repetitive nature of work (Deery and Kinnie, 2004; Houlihan, 2004), and various HR practices like the provision of a range of financial incentives, adoption of comprehensive recruitment strategies and the position of good promotional and career development policies are suggested as potential solutions (Budhwar et al., 2006).

2
The Call Centre Industry in India

The call centre industry in India is located within the country's emerging ITES–BPO sector whose major constituent is global off-shoring operations (henceforth also termed offshoring in this book).[1] The growth of offshoring in India has generated fierce debate. As Cohen and El-Sawad (2007) maintain, on a macro level, while some commentators have described such arrangements as providing hitherto unknown opportunities for economic and social prosperity, security and freedom, others see India as a source of cheap labour and this form of modernization as ultimately leading to even greater inequality. On a more micro level, commentators are similarly divided, with arguments that this sector is offering high wages and unprecedented career prospects to impressionable young people set against a view of Indian customer service workers as 'insecure' and 'vulnerable' casualties of the new economic order. Following a description of the sector, this chapter presents existing literature on the Indian call centre industry.

---

[1] In this book, the terms offshored and offshoring are henceforth used describe the relocation of services from developed to developing low cost countries (in this case, from USA [United States of America, also abbreviated as US]/UK [United Kingdom]/Australia/Canada to India). The terms subcontractor and subcontracted are used to describe intra-country outsourcing to a third party service provider while the term in-house is used to describe service provision with the parent organization.

India's ITES–BPO Sector

Sectoral Overview

India's ITES–BPO sector encompasses the offshoring of such processes that can be enabled with information technology (NASSCOM, 2003) including in its ambit both call centres and back-office services. The figures provided by NASSCOM, the trade body and chamber of commerce for India's ITES–BPO sector,[2] are undeniably impressive (Table 2.1). ITES–BPO exports were estimated to have grown from USD (United States Dollar) 1.5 billion in 2001–02 to USD 6.3 billion in 2005–06, while revenue in domestic ITES–BPO grew from USD 0.6 billion to USD 0.9 billion from 2004–05 to 2005–06 (NASSCOM, 2006).

According to NASSCOM (2006), the key catalyst of Indian ITES–BPO export is globalization. The rapid spread of globalization

TABLE 2.1 Indian ITES–BPO Export Revenues

Financial Year	USD Billion
1999–2000	0.6
2000–01	0.9
2001–02	1.5
2002–03	2.5
2003–04	3.1
2004–05	4.6
2005–06 (estimate)	6.3

Source: NASSCOM, 2006: 262.

---

[2] NASSCOM is India's National Association of Software and Service Companies, the premier trade body and the chamber of commerce of the IT software and services industry in India. As of 31 December 2005, NASSCOM had over 950 members, of which over 150 are global companies from the US, UK, EU (European Union), Japan and China. NASSCOM's member companies are in the business of software development, software services, software products and ITES–BPO services. A not-for-profit organization, NASSCOM's primary objective is to act as a catalyst for the growth of the software-driven IT industry in India. Other goals include facilitation of trade and business in software and services, encouragement and advancement of research, propagation of education and employment, enabling the growth of the Indian economy and provision of compelling business benefits to global economies via global sourcing (NASSCOM, 2006).

has added competitive pressure across geographic markets impacting growth and profitability. This has pushed organizations towards cost-efficient business models resulting in global offshoring. Today global offshoring is a key element in the business strategy of organizations and has moved beyond mere functional support. India, thanks to her demonstrated superiority, sustained cost advantage and powered value propositions, has emerged as the main global beneficiary of this project. Offshoring to India has provided companies around the world with significant benefits in terms of labour arbitrage. Apart from providing organizations with annual cost savings of 40 to 50 per cent as compared to the annual wage inflation of 10 to 15 per cent, such operations also leverage declines in telecom costs and other overheads while at the same time enhancing productivity. The large English-speaking and technical talent pool available in India is the critical component in this process. Over 44,000 engineering degree and diploma holders, approximately 2.3 million other (arts, commerce and science) graduates and 300,000 post-graduates are added to the workforce each year. NASSCOM (2006) points out that India's numerous advantages have resulted in a steady increase in the scale and depth of existing service lines and in the addition of newer vertical-specific and emerging, niche business services, fuelling the growth of this sector. Indeed, that, globally, India is considered to be a competent and valued offshoring destination is borne out by the growing trend of locating higher value knowledge-based processes here, in addition to the existing lower end business processes (NASSCOM, 2006).

Budhwar et al. (2006) cite data to highlight why India has become the electronic housekeeper of the world. The main reasons for the rapid growth of call centres include the availability of over 2 million English-speaking graduates every year who are ready to work at up to 80 per cent less salary than their Western counterparts, availability of technical and computer literate human resources, enormous savings for foreign firms by offshoring their processes to India, availability of useful infrastructure such as established telecom services, better productivity and quality of services (many Indian call centres have successfully adopted several industry standards such as Software Engineering Institute–Capability Maturity Model [SEI–CMM], International Standards Organization [ISO], Total Quality Management [TQM], Six Sigma Quality and Customer Operations Performance Centre

[COPC]), secure environment (Indian call centres are adopting standards such as ISO17799, BS [British Standards] 7799, Control Objectives for Information and related Technology [COBIT] and IT Services Management [ITSM]), increased focus on core competencies and cheap costs to set up new offices. For example, an entry level staff member in India earns between USD 150 and USD 250 per month, which results in annual savings of USD 30,000 for every call centre employee. On a comparative note, for an average operation which takes 20 seconds to process in a US (USA/United States of America) facility, Indian call centres claim to handle it in just 8 seconds. In comparison to the UK, Indian call centres claim to have a much higher rate of error-free transactions. Infrastructural savings are also considerable. For instance, the cost of a recently built new call centre for Standard Chartered Bank in Chennai was GBP (Great Britain Pound) 19 million—a fraction of constructing a similar building in the Western world.

Dossani and Kenney (2003) support the aforementioned claims, pointing out that substantial cost savings combined with high quality services serve as the main drivers for offshoring, being facilitated by low labour costs, technological advances and project management skills. They quote NASSCOM data to show that in India, the direct costs per employee are USD 10,354 (or USD 5.20 per billable hour, of which USD 3.10 is the estimated labour cost). This is in contrast to the US, where the direct costs per employee are USD 55,598 (or USD 27.80 per billable hour, of which USD 21.50 is the estimated labour cost).

Locating India within the global space, NASSCOM–McKinsey (2005) calculates that India accounts for 46 per cent of offshored ITES–BPO, an increase from 39 per cent in 2001. Thus, India has captured an increasing share of the expanding global ITES–BPO industry. Further, this report estimates that, going forward, India can continue to grow its offshore IT and ITES–BPO industries at an annual rate of 25 per cent. By 2010, these industries combined could generate export revenues of about USD 60 billion.

The role of the Indian government in facilitating the growth and development of the country's ITES–BPO sector cannot be denied, with the liberalization of the Indian economy proving to be a critical turning point. According to NASSCOM (2006), from 1991 onwards, the Indian government has encouraged in-flow of foreign capital not only as a source of finance but also as a facilitator of knowledge and technology transfer. Today, foreign direct investment (FDI) in most sectors is permitted under the automatic route and only requires notification of India's central bank, the Reserve Bank of India (RBI). Procedures relating to the transfer of shares, repatriation and induction of foreign technology have been made simple. The procedures governing approval are continuously reviewed and updated to ensure ease of operationalization.

With specific reference to the ITES–BPO sector, support for its growth and development has emerged from various government ministries and departments, particularly the Ministry of Communication and Information Technology which has formulated policy and legal frameworks to facilitate the process. The policies promoted by India's central and state governments have been critical in creating favourable environments for foreign investors and domestic companies. The implementation of a series of incentives, concessions, subsidies and simplification of procedural requirements has served as an appropriate catalyst (NASSCOM, 2006). As NASSCOM (2006: 216–31) highlights, these include relaxation of policies relating to inbound and outbound investments, exchange control relaxations, incentives for units located in a domestic tariff area (DTA) or under export-oriented units (EOU)/software technology parks (STP)/special economic zones (SEZ) and electronic hardware technology park (EHTP) schemes, and state level incentives, waivers and subsidies.

Most state governments in India have announced special promotional schemes for the ITES–BPO sector. These schemes focus on the key issues of infrastructure, electronic governance and IT education and on providing a facilitating environment for increasing IT proliferation in the respective states. While these are state-specific initiatives, there is a fair degree of uniformity across the various states as newer locations have modelled their schemes on those offered in states that have successfully nurtured a thriving ITES–BPO industry (NASSCOM, 2006).

The Indian ITES–BPO industry has grown despite serious constraints posed by infrastructure including road systems, public transport, electrical power supply, telecommunications connectivity, etc., across Tier-1, Tier-2 and Tier-3 cities. Taylor and Bain (2003b) believe that

India's huge labour cost advantage is offset by greater proportional costs in relation to, amongst other things, equipment, telephony, telecommunications connectivity and power supply. In the case of the latter two components, the inescapable requirement to provide 'redundancy', that is alternative provision, adds significantly to the cost base of Indian suppliers. They go on to state that though NASSCOM consistently estimates that overall cost savings of 40 to 50 per cent can be realized by offshoring business processes to India (NASSCOM, 2006), such a stand represents optimism and oversimplification since a variety of factors including the nature of the process, the degree of complexity, the scale and volume of the activity, the nature and terms of the contract and the stage of the migratory cycle impact the level of achievable savings (Taylor and Bain, 2006).

Organizational Landscape

In contractual terms, a variety of engagement models depict the relationship between the Indian/India-based service provider and the entity seeking services (henceforth also referred to as the client in this book)[3]. While engagement models range from joint ventures, captives and third-party dedicated centres to build-operate-transfer (BOT), the BOT model is becoming popular. Here, the client contracts with a service provider to undertake a process in a dedicated manner and acquire it once an agreed scale and scope has been achieved. The BOT model is gaining preference as it offers clients the ability to leverage the third party service provider's process expertise and efficient cost structure, lower transition time and maintain a relatively higher degree of control on the offshored operation (NASSCOM, 2006).

From the range of pricing models available (including per unit time/variable pricing per seat/per hour; per seat or full-time employee (FTE) per month; activity-based billing; gain-share models; and hybrid-pricing models), the per unit time/variable pricing model is the one most frequently adopted by Indian ITES–BPO companies (NASSCOM, 2006).

---

[3] The reader must note the distinction between clients and customers. Clients are entities seeking services from Indian/India-based service providers while customers are the clients' service recipients who by virtue of being served by the agents/employees/CSRs of the service provider are also referred to by the latter as customers.

Taylor and Bain (2006) highlight the gradual emergence of the global service delivery model where some Indian ITES–BPO firms are attempting to expand beyond Indian borders either organically or via acquisitions to establish their presence in multiple geographies, not just imitating the strategy of existing multinational corporations (MNCs) such as IBM, Accenture, etc., and captives such as HSBC, etc., but also serving as competition for them. The adoption of a global service delivery model is seen as advantageous because, firstly, it allows service providers and clients to 'follow the sun', and secondly, it enables service providers and clients to access and capitalize on the resources and competences available in and specific to different geographies. In addition, complex dynamics within the Indian context including annual compensation increases that make talent more expensive and increasing demand from non-English language belts as well as the presence of low cost, highly educated workforces in other nations influence this trend (Bhasin in NASSCOM, 2005a). Of course, as Taylor and Bain (2006) observe, this shift remains uneven with many firms having neither the resources nor the inclination to establish multisite, multigeography set-ups.

The distinction within India's ITES–BPO industry in terms of types of organizations reveals its heterogeneous nature. 'Captives', essentially in-house service providers for global companies (for example, HSBC, Dell, Hewlett Packard, Prudential), which directly own and control their offshored operations and dominated the industry in its early years, remain pre-eminent, according to NASSCOM (2005a: 90). 'Third party MNCs', that is, MNCs operating out of India that essentially act as third party service providers with a broad portfolio of business processes delivering services for their clients, form another category. Both these types can be distinguished from 'Indian third party' service providers which act as classic offshore operations. This diverse category encompasses both what are known as 'pure plays' (Indian companies providing voice or non-voice or both services to clients in specific and multiple sectors and geographies overseas—for example, Transworks or Firstsource) and the 'ITES–BPO arms of Indian IT companies' such as Wipro or Infosys. Finally, it is important to take account of the more recent emergence and significant expansion in the 'domestic ITES–BPO sub-sector' (NASSCOM, 2005a).

Dossani and Kenney (2003) cover the same range of organizations as does NASSCOM (2005a) above, but engage two criteria, namely, whether they are Indian or multinational owned and operated and whether they are a captive firm or a third-party firm. Their categorization, though ideographically subsuming the same organizations as NASSCOM (2005a), nomothetically includes MNC captives, MNC outsourcers, MNC specialists, non-resident Indian (NRI) firms, Indian specialists, Indian independents, Indian IT subsidiaries and Indian non-IT subsidiaries. In Dossani and Kenney's (2003) view, the relatively nascent stage of the Indian ITES–BPO sector makes it difficult to predict which organizational form will become dominant.

While the principal location for the ITES–BPO industry remains Tier-1 cities, namely, New Delhi and the National Capital Region (NCR), Mumbai, Bangalore, Chennai and Hyderabad, there has been considerable expansion of operations into Tier-2 and Tier-3 cities and towns in the last three years. Pune was the first Tier-2 city to emerge as a major location for ITES–BPO as companies such as Convergys, WNS, Progeon, EXL and MphasiS established operations. Examples of newer locations and the companies who have situated these operations in the last year include the following: Mangalore (MphasiS), Vishakhapatnam (Satyam, Wipro, TCS, HSBC), Madurai (Honeywell), Nagpur (Krishna Group), Chandigarh (Infosys, IBM–Daksh), Jaipur (GE), Kochi (Wipro, OPI) and Thiruvananthapuram (Infosys) (NASSCOM, 2006: 94). Tier-2 and Tier-3 locations offer both talent pools as well as lower cost structures besides reducing organizational risk through geographical dispersion and enabling utilization of state government sponsored financial and other assistance schemes (NASSCOM, 2005a and 2006). Indeed, so rapid has been the growth of some Tier-2 locations that they have come to resemble Tier-1 cities in terms of overheated labour markets, rising costs and overstretched infrastructure, reinforcing the search for and development of new business districts beyond the boundaries unencumbered by these constraints (NASSCOM–McKinsey, 2005). Amidst this development is a group of organizations that remain undecided whether the advantages of locating in Tier-2 or Tier-3 cities sufficiently outweigh the benefits of continuing to remain in the established places. The view here is that relocation to Tier-2 and Tier-3 cities provides temporary relief but does not address critical issues within the industry particularly those relating to employee competence and retention and other HR difficulties (Taylor and Bain, 2006).

Nature of Work

While NASSCOM has not disaggregated call centre activity from back-office activity in the Indian ITES–BPO sector, Taylor and Bain (2006) maintain that, based on a review of all available evidence, it is reasonable to conclude that voice services account for 60 to 65 per cent of sectoral employment and the various back-office activities for 35 to 40 per cent, although a proportion of employees are employed in both types of activities. They go on to state that offshored services are essentially lower end, encompassing basic voice services and simple transactional business processes which are highly standardized and routinized. Indeed, Taylor and Bain (2006: 49) hold that this can be ascertained by the preponderance of voice services, that is, '...the greater the proportion of voice services in the Indian market then the more that section of the ITES–BPO industry remains concentrated at a relatively standardized level'. In their view, it is limited facility with conversational English that inhibits participation in the provision of more complex services.

Finance and accounting (F&A), customer interaction services (CIS) and human resource (HR) administration are key service categories, accounting for 89 per cent of industry revenues. F&A services manage or support aspects of the finance and accounting functions of businesses. This includes activities such as general accounting, transaction management (accounts receivables and payables management), corporate finance (for example, treasury and risk management and tax management), compliance management and statutory reporting. This segment accounts for approximately 40 per cent of Indian ITES–BPO. The CIS segment, which comprises all forms of IT-enabled customer contact such as inbound or outbound and voice or non-voice based support used to provide customer services, sales and marketing and technical support and help desk services, accounts for approximately 46 per cent of Indian ITES–BPO. HR administration services such as payroll and benefits administration, travel and expense processing, talent acquisition and talent management services, employee and manager self-service delivery services and employee communication design and administration accounts for approximately 3 per cent of

Indian ITES–BPO. Within these, banking, financial services and insurance (BFSI) is among the most mature vertical, estimated to account for approximately 35 to 45 per cent of offshored ITES–BPO and possessing the greatest service line depth (NASSCOM, 2006).

Emerging vertical-specific and niche business services being delivered from India, which are estimated to account for 11 per cent of the total value of ITES–BPO activity undertaken in India, include financial services research support and analysis for equity/debt/derivatives markets (e.g., professionals in India supporting a team of financial analysts on Wall Street in equity/debt research, investment and fund management activities), econometrics, data analytics and modelling, business/corporate research/competitive intelligence, pharmaceutical/health care/life science, legal services, animation and game development services, medical transcription and basic, shared back-office and administrative functions (NASSCOM, 2006).

Claims have been made that in a bid to stave off competition from other geographies, the industry is moving up the value chain through diversification from call centre work to back-office processes that are complex and of higher value. While these claims are rooted in actual developments, they are still frequently exaggerated and relatively standardized call centre services continue to dominate. Moreover, growing back-office work involves routine standardized work largely, with only a slightly higher proportion of complex higher value processes than what was present earlier. One exception remains the emerging knowledge process outsourcing (KPO) which entails genuine complexity and high value services. KPO includes service providers with higher end research and analytic-based services in both traditional service lines and new business areas. Unlike conventional back-office work where the focus is on process expertise, in KPO, the focus is on knowledge expertise and on advanced technical and analytical skills. Engineers, Masters in Business Administration (MBAs), PhDs (Doctors of Philosophy), Chartered Financial Analysts (CFAs), lawyers, etc., are groups sought after for employment in KPO organizations. Moreover, KPO solutions are more likely to be customized, rather than standardized as is the case with traditional back-office work. Concomitant with this is the understanding that customers are looking for focus rather than breadth or size, and therefore, will be looking for those KPO service providers who have the necessary expertise, depth and experience (Taylor and Bain, 2006).

Perhaps the emphasis on lower end processes is to enable the delivery of higher volumes and, in turn, the realization of scale economics particularly in the current context of rising costs, sharpened competition and declining margins. While KPO activities can deliver higher returns, they are limited in scale by customization requirements (Taylor and Bain, 2006).

Employment Patterns

Direct employment in India's ITES–BPO sector (not including employment in the IT industry) was calculated at 553,000 for 2006–07. Presenting figures in Table 2.2 as provided by NASSCOM, the rapid growth of the ITES–BPO industry in India is obvious (Taylor et al., 2007).

TABLE 2.2   Indian ITES–BPO Employment Levels

Financial Year	Employees ('000s)	% Year on Year Increase
2001–02	107	n/a
2002–03	171	60
2003–04[a]	216	26
2004–05[a]	316	46
2005–06	409	29
2006–07[b]	553	35

Source: Taylor et al. 2007, based on data from NASSCOM, 2003: 59; 2006: 73; 2007a.
Notes: [a]The totals have been recalculated to exclude certain service lines.
[b]Figures presented at NASSCOM ITES–BPO Strategy Summit in Bangalore in August 2007 (NASSCOM, 2007a).

Offshoring to India is driven by labour cost arbitrage. It is believed that the ability to achieve such high levels of cost advantage by seeking services from India essentially emerges because of the availability of highly skilled talent at significantly lower wage costs and the resultant productivity gains derived from having a very competent employee base. The advantages of cheap labour primarily arise because of their ability to speak English, an indispensable prerequisite for an industry serving English-speaking geographies. There is no question that facility with the English language distinguishes India from some alternative offshoring locations. Indeed, there is an ample supply of graduates of universities and colleges with at least 15 years education in English

(NASSCOM, 2006). The industrial relations climate perceived to characterize the Indian ITES–BPO sector adds on to the attractiveness of the labour market. That is, it is widely believed across the country by society at large that the ITES–BPO sector does not fall within the purview of existing labour laws. As discussed in the following paragraphs, this view is maintained and promoted by employers within the sector and supported by government apathy. Taylor and Bain (2003b) assert that India is attractive to organizations who wish to capitalize on the possibilities for flexible labour utilization. They point out that given the absence of trade unions in the Indian ITES–BPO sector, offshoring offers an opportunity to deliver services in an industrial relations environment in which organizations are less constrained by the need to consult with workforce representatives (Taylor and Bain, 2003b).

In assessing the labour-related advantages offered by India, Taylor and Bain (2003b and 2006) caution that participation in 15 years of education in English does not automatically prepare the workforce to interact effectively with remote customers for whom English is the mother tongue. That is, while agents' formal command of English is largely satisfactory, they do not possess the depth of understanding and flexibility of expression to ensure that more than routine tasks can be performed. Furthermore, some commentators have suggested that despite efforts by Indian organizations, the deep-rooted cultural differences between India and the West might adversely affect interaction between agents and customers (Taylor and Bain, 2003b).

Moreover, there is absolutely no doubt that the ITES–BPO workforce is covered under existing labour legislation (see Noronha and D'Cruz, 2008a). Under the Constitution of India, labour falls under the concurrent list which implies that both the central and the state governments are competent to enact related legislations, subject to certain matters being reserved for the centre's jurisdiction such that in cases of conflict, the provisions of the centre prevail. In the context of ITES–BPO organizations, the relevant state legislation is the Shops and Commercial Establishments Act as promulgated in various Indian states while the central legislations are the Workmen's Compensation Act (1923), the Payment of Wages Act (1936), the Industrial Disputes Act (1947), the Minimum Wages Act (1948), the Employees State Insurance Act (1948), the Maternity Benefit Act (1961), the Contract

Labour (Regulation and Abolition) Act (1970), the Payment of Gratuity Act (1972) and the Equal Remuneration Act (1976).

However, as highlighted earlier, the popular notion held in Indian society (and maintained and promoted by ITES–BPO employers, aided by government apathy) is that the aforementioned legislations and related institutional measures do not apply to this sector, and hence ITES–BPO employees do not come under the purview of the labour laws applicable to blue-collared workers. That some scholars believe that the Shops and Commercial Establishments Act became a passive instrument once ITES–BPO organizations in most of Indian states were granted the status of 'public utility service' providers under the Industrial Disputes Act, 1947, echoes the popular view (see, for example, Banerjee, 2006). To clarify the ensuing confusion, India's labour minister confirmed in Parliament that ITES–BPO organizations were covered under existing labour laws and the state governments were the 'appropriate government' legally vested with powers to deal with violations of these laws in the sector (Rajya Sabha Unstarred Question Number 2526 answered on 21 March 2007 and Lok Sabha Starred Question Number 374 answered on 10 September 2007). Our discussions with labour commissioners across five Indian states were in line with the Minister's position (See Noronha and D'Cruz, 2008a). In reality, then, none of the ITES–BPO organizations have been granted 'public utility service' status as per the Industrial Disputes Act, 1947. The only exemptions granted by various state governments pertain to their respective Shops and Commercial Establishments Acts. Accordingly, the state governments have exempted ITES–BPO organizations from some of the provisions of the Shops and Commercial Establishments Act that allow the ITES–BPO companies to run their operations round the clock, on all seven days of the week, 365 days of the year, employing women at all times. In other words, ITES–BPO organizations have been provided with exemptions relating to opening and closing hours and employment of women beyond the time limits mentioned in the Shops and Commercial Establishments Act, subject to the requisite security and transport facilities being provided to them by the employer organization (Noronha and D'Cruz, 2008a).

Further, it is important to note that rising labour costs, conservatively estimated at the rate of 10 to 15 per cent per annum for the last three years

(NASSCOM, 2006), emerging essentially due to wage inflation, have eaten into cost savings. High and rising rates of attrition are significant here. Indian companies appear to be paying higher salaries in order to retain existing staff or to be recruiting from a labour pool in which competitive pressures are intensifying. High attrition has the added effect of increasing recruitment and training budgets. The supply of experienced and competent Indian call centre agents, at unchanging cost levels, cannot therefore be regarded as inexhaustible (Taylor and Bain, 2003b). Taylor and Bain (2006) point out that these rising labour costs vary across the country and across processes while also being higher for management as compared to employees. There are additional aspects of the cost base in India which might not appear obvious at first sight. The expenses incurred in the complex and extensive logistical exercise of transporting agents to the call centre workplace and the provision of free or subsidized food, among other things, are significant additional costs which have to be borne by Indian employers. For all these reasons, the spectacular savings which prima facie appear to be offered in India, when labour costs are assessed in isolation, are qualified in practice (Taylor and Bain, 2003b).

Nonetheless, NASSCOM (2006) maintains that India continues to remain the most cost competitive sourcing base for ITES–BPO offshoring. Despite rising wages with increasing labour costs being offset by declining telecom costs, lower depreciation and other infrastructure costs, improvements in productivity and utilization and scale economies allow India to sustain her cost advantage. Indeed, the attempt to sustain the long-term viability of India's cost advantage has resulted in the adoption of various tactics and strategies including increasing company size and facilities such that an increased volume of processes can be handled as well as management of productivity through reengineering and optimal use of equipment and labour such that efficiencies can be leveraged upon. To help institutionalize the concept of process excellence in the industry, NASSCOM is, in association with several agencies, developing a benchmarking service to provide companies with a robust framework for self-assessment that may be administered at regular intervals such that benchmarks of industry performance for meaningful comparison and subsequent action may be obtained. Movement to Tier-2 and Tier-3 cities is also seen as lowering costs of labour, infrastructure and overheads

(NASSCOM, 2006). Beyond organization-level initiatives, government and industry are working towards increasing labour supply, improving infrastructure and providing an enabling environment. In addition, process superiority is also seen as driving significant savings from improvements in quality, speed and flexibility, productivity and delivery innovation (NASSCOM, 2006).

Despite infrastructure problems and labour-related challenges, various studies (including those by the McKinsey Global Institute Survey and A.T. Kearney) maintain that India remains the offshoring destination of choice, delivering the best bundle of benefits globally. India has successfully leveraged its fundamental advantages of abundant talent, a keen focus on quality and low cost, coupled with an enabling business environment to attain the leadership position in this space (NASSCOM, 2006). Yet, in the words of Taylor and Bain (2006: 47):

> ...the pressure on the cost base, particularly from rising labour costs, is set to continue, and is likely to prove more significant in its impact than the combined counter-effect of all the cost reduction measures, and the anticipated further decline in telecom costs. In other words, India will remain an attractive destination because of its low cost base, but in overall terms the slow erosion of the cost differential seems set to continue.

In overall terms, then, the ITES–BPO industry in India still tends to provide largely standardized, routinized services of generally low complexity, despite limited moves up the value chain to KPO (Taylor and Bain, 2006). Accordingly, it has been demonstrated that the work system in Indian call centres largely approximates, and indeed may well constitute, an exaggerated form of the mass production model (Batt et al., 2005a; Taylor and Bain, 2005).

Working in India's Call Centres

India's ITES–BPO sector has emerged as an important avenue for employment, especially for the country's youth. As Ramesh (2004) and McMillin (2006) show, the average age of call centre employees is 25 years, with the main age bracket being 21 to 25 years. Even managers in call centres belong to a lower age bracket, with Mehta et al. (2006)

indicating an average age of 31.6 years. Similarly, Budhwar et al. (2006) point out that the average age of junior management ranges between 20 to 26 years, while for middle management, the range is between 24 to 32 years. The average age for senior management is 45 years. High levels of education characterize those entering this industry. Ramesh's (2004) finding that 97 per cent of call centre agents are graduates was confirmed by Batt et al. (2005a) and Budhwar et al. (2006) who reported about 15 years of formal education or a basic undergraduate degree. Indeed, the level of education of agents in India compared favourably to those of the agents in the US. The typical worker in an Indian call centre had 14 years of education (on an average, two years of college) compared to 13.3 years among US in-house establishments and 12.6 years for US subcontractors where the typical worker had an average education of a high school diploma only (Batt et al., 2005b).

In the sections which follow, we present the findings of earlier empirical research on working in Indian call centres. It is relevant to mention that these inquiries have been located in MNC captive, MNC third-party and Indian third-party call centres (henceforth also referred to as international facing call centres since both clients and customers are located overseas) and focus on employee experiences, though managerial views may sometimes be included.

Recruitment and Training

Recruitment of call centre agents takes place through walk-in/telephonic interviews, placement agencies, call centre colleges and referrals, and involves written tests, group discussions, aptitude tests and tests of communication skills and language ability (McMillin, 2006; Ramesh, 2004). Displaying fluency with spoken and written English, ability to multitask, having computer skills, possessing a pleasant voice, ability to be persuasive, having a positive approach, good communication skills, neutral accent, good attitude, higher energy levels and being a quick learner were qualities that were valued by call centres while selecting employees (Batt et al., 2005a; McMillin, 2006; Ramesh, 2004).

Once recruited, training forms an important component of the call centre set-up and encompasses a four week to eight week period (Ramesh, 2004). Training activities receive at least 25 per cent of the organization's budget (Budhwar et al., 2006) and include generic (such as cultural and linguistic training, communication skills and emotional labour skills) and process-specific modules. These modules could be conducted by in-house trainers and experienced agents or be subcontracted to adult education sites where individuals themselves pay for the training they receive (Budhwar et al., 2006; McMillin, 2006; Mirchandani, 2004; Ramesh, 2004). While making comparisons with the US, Batt et al. (2005b) state that the initial training in US subcontracted centres is less than half of that found in Indian offshored centres but once cultural and linguistic training is accounted for, it appears that Indian centres do not provide more initial training for other aspects of the job. Post-training, employees in Indian offshored call centres take 13 weeks to become proficient on the job (Batt et al., 2005b). Similarly, the amount of on-the-job training and the annual rates of on-going training are not substantially different with offshored call centres providing 4.7 weeks on an average and in-house call centres providing 3.9 weeks on an average. However, investment in on-going training does not appear to be sufficient, given the high demand for new skills and information processing required by such jobs (Batt et al., 2005b). Following training, agents 'go live' and are on three-month probation, and depending on their performance, decisions are made about confirmation and/or retention (McMillin, 2006). By and large, call centres in India employ permanent employees as compared to part-timers in the West. In fact, part-time and temporary workers form only a very small employee group in call centre organizations in India (Budhwar et al., 2006).

Work Systems and Job Design

Stringent controls form part and parcel of work life in the call centre. ICTs facilitate pacing of work, monitoring, surveillance and maintenance of archival records, giving rise to and/or allowing for the use of numerous quantitative and qualitative performance measures (Ramesh, 2004). These measures place substantial limits on employees' ability to use their discretion on the job. Batt et al. (2005b) conclude that despite relying on a more educated and full-time workforce, Indian call centres have work systems that are more tightly constrained and standardized than those found among US subcontracted or in-house call centres. With the exception of reliance on scripts, which is higher in the US subcontracted call centres, Indian call centre managers report substantially lower levels of discretion given to agents over handling customer requests and use of problem-solving groups. Indeed, mechanisms that facilitate employee participation in management decisions and problem-solving groups, which improve employee morale and performance as well as facilitate knowledge sharing and stymie attrition, were found to be very low in Indian call centres. Low levels of discretion also apply to pacing work, scheduling rest breaks and handling unexpected customer requests/complaints (Batt et al., 2005b). Call centre employees work in shifts of 8 to 9.5 hours, which have three breaks (Ramesh, 2004). The two tea/coffee breaks are of 15 minutes each while the lunch/dinner break is of 30 minutes (D'Cruz and Noronha, 2008). The total break time did not exceed 60 minutes. However, breaks were decided by the TLs on the basis of call levels or call queues (McMillin, 2006; Noronha and D'Cruz, 2006). Unscheduled breaks during working hours were not permitted while scheduled breaks were tracked by specially designed software. Leave records were also meticulously tracked. Availing of leave, including sick leave, required prior intimation to and consent from management so that work was not interrupted (Noronha and D'Cruz, 2006).

Performance-based data (which include the amount of leave an employee has availed of), besides being used to determine compensation, increments, promotions and training needs, was consolidated over time and publicly displayed. Employees who topped performance charts were considered role models while those at the bottom were provided with assistance by way of training and feedback (Budhwar et al., 2006; Ramesh, 2004). Those failing to show marked improvement in performance faced dismissal. Apart from performance-related reasons, the threat of being dismissed remained omnipresent, heightening employment insecurities. The combination of all these forms of control resulted in constant stress for agents (Ramesh, 2004).

Work also got frustrating, especially when dealing with abusive customers. Even the most positive and alert agents report that there were times when they lost their temper and had to cry or curse in order to vent their frustration (Ramesh, 2004). Being targets of racism further complicated the situation. It was not uncommon for customers to accuse agents of depriving them of their jobs, to refuse to speak to Indians or to insist on speaking to someone who knew English. These caustic interactions precipitated strain in agents (D'Cruz and Noronha, 2006 and 2008; McMillin, 2006).

Agents thus work in highly segmented environments akin to Fordist/Taylorist assembly lines (Ramesh, 2004). Organizations seemed to be adopting a tightly controlled, cost-efficient, bureaucratic and customer-oriented structure resulting in monotonous work (Budhwar et al., 2006; Noronha and D'Cruz, 2007). It was, therefore, not surprising to note that call centres came to be called 'new-age sweatshops' or 'captive units' (Budhwar et al., 2006) or an exaggerated form of a mass production model (Batt et al., 2005a; Taylor and Bain, 2005) while agents working there were called 'cyber coolies' (Ramesh, 2004).

This work context, according to Batt et al. (2005b), explains the high attrition rates in subcontracted and offshored call centres as compared to in-house call centres. Subcontracted and offshored call centres were more constrained to follow standardized operating procedures and performance monitoring. What is particularly striking in the case of India is that work and employment systems exhibit contradictory characteristics. On one hand, employees have high levels of formal education and receive pay that is considerably above the national market wage. On the other hand, these same highly qualified individuals receive few or no opportunities to use those skills because the work is designed to limit independent decision-making or innovative problem-solving. Employers are thus paying for skills without making effective use of them. Moreover, quitting becomes the preferred option for call centre employees who are dissatisfied with their jobs and who do not see prospects for better opportunities in their current organizations. Besides job design and limited growth and career development opportunities, Budhwar et al. (2006) outline that difficulty with customers, inadequate job enrichment, burnout stress syndrome (BOSS), better pay and incentives offered by other companies, employees pursuing higher studies, favouritism in appraisals and promotions, a closed management system and health and psychological ailments arising out of night shifts result in employee frustration, and ultimately, resignation.

Personal and Social Life

Typically, call centres operate round the clock all through the year (that is, 24/7/365), relying on night shifts to service overseas geographies whose time zones are ahead or behind that of India (McMillin, 2006; Noronha and D'Cruz, 2006; Ramesh, 2004). This was identified by many call centre agents as the most difficult part of their jobs, thus reflecting the fundamental immobility of time and their continued embeddedness within their local social contexts (Mirchandani, 2004). Odd working hours usually led to disturbance in personal and social life. There were problems related to maintaining friendships, keeping in touch with relatives, accomplishing household duties and finding time for sound family relations (McMillin, 2006; Mirchandani, 2004; Noronha and D'Cruz, 2006; Poster, 2007; Ramesh, 2004; Singh and Pandey, 2005). This situation was exacerbated by constant change in shifts, making agents having to continuously adjust to new work times and significantly impacting their health (Mirchandani, 2004), as manifest in several symptoms of mental and physical illness such as nervousness, chronic fatigue, stiff neck, sore eyes, backaches and headaches, impaired vision, numbness in fingers, body ache, fever, asthma, sore throats, nausea, dizziness, rashes, insomnia, anxiety, restlessness, irritability, depression, drowsiness, loss of appetite, changes in body weight, decreasing vigilance and gastrointestinal problems (McMillin, 2006; Noronha and D'Cruz, 2006; Poster, 2007; Ramesh, 2004). It was also noticed that agents develop poor eating habits, overeating, smoking and drinking excessive coffee and so on to cope up with the psychological and physical strain (McMillin, 2006; Ramesh, 2004; Singh and Pandey, 2005). In short, employees have much to lose in this scenario of transnational call centre work. They stand to compromise their bodies, their mental stability, their family lives as well as their career trajectories (Poster, 2007).

Remuneration and Working Conditions

Indian call centres pay a competitive compensation package as compared to the remuneration available in other sectors of the Indian economy such as factory work, secretarial work and teaching, at times enabling agents to earn more than their parents (Budhwar et al., 2006; D'Cruz and Noronha, 2006; Poster, 2007). Nonetheless, researchers here found variations in salaries. Mitter et al. (2004) found the average initial salary for call centre agents to be approximately Indian Rupees (Rs) 8,000 per month which increased to Rs 12,000 per month within a year. Trainers got around Rs 15,000 to Rs 18,000 per month and managers got Rs 35,000 to Rs 45,000 per month. Ramesh (2004) shows that 53 per cent of call centre employees receive a monthly salary of Rs 10,000 or more while 19 per cent received between Rs 8,000 to Rs 10,000 per month. Further, McMillin's (2006) findings reveal that 66 per cent of the employees at the agent level earned between Rs 5,000 to Rs 10,000 per month, though 20 per cent of this group earned between Rs 10,000 to Rs 15,000 per month.

Moreover, Batt et al. (2005b) found a difference of 30 per cent in the annual pay (including basic and performance-related pay except overtime) received by Indian agents employed by international facing call centres (Rs 1,21,444) as compared to their counterparts employed in India's domestic call centres (Rs 94,861).

What is also relevant is that though Indian call centre employees are better educated than their Western counterparts, they are paid less than the latter. Batt et al. (2005b) found that the average median annual pay reported by call centre managers is USD 27,713 among in-house call centres, USD 23,881 in subcontracted US centres, and USD 2,635 in offshored centres. Thus, in-house call centres pay about 14 per cent more than subcontracted centres, and 90 per cent more than the offshored segment. Nonetheless, though these salaries may seem small by American or British standards, they provide a high quality of life to agents in India (Mitter et al., 2004). Materially, Indian agents gain employment opportunities, upgraded pay and comfortable working conditions (Poster, 2007).

Besides high salaries, call centre organizations offer facilities like reading rooms, internet browsing centres, gymnasiums, free transportation after night shifts, free or subsidized meals, games facilities, medical facilities and recreational and cultural activities such as get-togethers and outings to break the routinization, monotony and pressures of the job (Ng and Mitter, 2005; Poster, 2007; Ramesh, 2004). Thus, there is an effort to project the workplace as a fun place (Ramesh, 2004). In addition, workers also gain secondary benefits like the status of working for a multinational firm and opportunities to visit client sites in foreign countries as part of training requirements (Poster, 2007).

In keeping with a stated emphasis on employee interests, call centre organizations manage employer–employee relations via open forum meetings, open door policies, intranet discussion fora, counselling, grievance procedures and suggestion schemes (Ramesh, 2004). Given this, some scholars argue that working conditions in Indian call centres are better than those of call centre firms in the US (Poster, 2007).

Moreover, international call centres in India are housed in clean, well-organized structures, which often have entrances decorated with glass and marble (Mirchandani, 2004). In short, what attracts people to this sector is the modern and Westernized environment manifested via the physical infrastructure, the fun element enmeshed with work, the state-of-the-art technology, the upwardly mobile peer group and colleagues, the perception of career prospects and the status associated with the job emerging from attractive remuneration, designations and work environment (D'Cruz and Noronha, 2006; McMillin, 2006; Ramesh, 2004; Singh and Pandey, 2005), reinforcing the view that a call centre job is highly desirable and highly skilled. Notwithstanding this, Ramesh (2004) argues that employers' espoused commitment to employee interests, as noted above, seems to be eclipsed by the primacy of management.

Cultural Dimensions

Indian call centre agents working in international facing call centres are expected to speak with accents, take on pseudonyms, adopt holidays and greetings, and work on Western time while masking their geographical location (D'Cruz and Noronha, 2008; Mirchandani, 2004). This, according to Patel (2006), represents a shift from exporting the production of material goods or culture to a full-scale reproduction of identity and culture. In the process, the range of employees' identity that is subject to managerial control is not just limited to emotions but to the whole unified sense of citizenship or nationality, which Poster (2007) refers to as national identity management. Given this requirement, a debate has ensued about the impact of ICTs and globalization on culture in terms of whether the development of ICTs would homogenize identities or reject the proposed standardized Northern identity. In this context, Poster (2007) argues that Indian call centre employees display responses that fall within this continuum combining elements of both homogenization and rejection, with most common responses being accommodation, objection, and resistance. Thus, despite the strategies by both clients and Indian service providers to enforce national identity requirements on agents in international facing call centres, the effect among employees is not a uniform assimilation into the acquired identity but instead various degrees of global disjuncture, dissent, and renegotiation in identities. Similarly, Mirchandani (2004) argues that the emulation of culture seldom brings about a straightforward cultural homogenization, with employees defying their construction as a passive and grateful workforce.

In contrast, while subscribing to this hybridization of culture thesis, McMillin (2006) believes that call centre labour is structured within an ideology of capitalist expansion and neo-colonialism. The system survives on complicity and subordination but so does the very existence and continuity of the call centre agents who work within this ideology, accepting their cultural subordination as part of the job, resulting in the cultural transformation of urban Indian labour into a global proletariat. This view, according to Cohen and El-Sawad (2007), seems to suggest that a new Western identity is being foisted on call centre employees which is not only at odds with their lives outside of work but which also amounts to them leading double lives (Ramesh, 2004). Cohen and El-Sawad (2007) argue against this kind of cultural takeover and highlight cultural ascriptions not as a window into agents' feelings about cultural identity, but as rhetorical devices used to justify certain patterns of thought and behaviour. In this sense, call centre employees could be seen as participating in the kind of invisibility and conditioning effects as part and parcel of the process of colonialism and its most recent expression in globalization (Cohen and El-Sawad, 2007).

Gender Issues

Researchers draw attention to the fact that the media representation of call centre employment in India as being primarily female is incorrect (Patel, 2006). Patel's (2006) findings that 60 per cent of Indian call centre employees are men coincides with those of Poster (2007) and Mirchandani (2003a) who found 50 to 70 per cent of Indian call centre employees to be men. Related to this, another myth that Patel (2006) endeavours to correct is that Indian society has finally accepted the possibility of women working at night (Singh and Pandey, 2005). Critiquing this, Patel (2006) argues that the emergence of this industry is not shifting patriarchal relations of power in a significant way, and social and spatial constraints on women's mobility in the urban nightscape continue. In other words, women's bodies continue to be marked as sites of transgression, and organizations put in considerable effort to convince society that women working at night occupy perfectly safe and decent work environments (Ng and Mitter, 2005). Besides this, domestic roles remain unchanged (Singh and Pandey, 2005).

Not surprisingly, then, the profile of the existing female workforce in Indian call centres is predominantly unmarried women, without many familial commitments (Ramesh, 2004), and the attrition of women agents is found to coincide with their engagement, marriage or pregnancy, restricting their career growth (McMillin, 2006; Ng and Mitter, 2005; Ramesh, 2004). In fact, women call centre agents who are above 30 years old and married generally have special circumstances such as being widowed/divorced, having grown-up children or being married to call centre managers/similar professionals (Ramesh, 2004). The other reason for the restricted growth of women in call centre organizations is the glass ceiling effect. Some researchers state that where there was no discrimination against women at the entry level, very few women attain managerial positions (McMillin, 2006; Singh and Pandey, 2005). Nonetheless, Ng and Mitter (2005) argue that this industry has accorded recognition and economic value to women's interpersonal skills which went unacknowledged earlier.

Managerial Concerns

Mehta et al. (2006) observe that the challenges reported by Indian call centre managers at various levels of the organization were different. Lower management concerns revolved around meeting targets, handling customers, managing work-life balance, dealing with competition and adapting to change. For middle management, relevant issues included motivating agents, handling attrition, achieving targets and maintaining employee and client satisfaction. Upper management focused on client demands, operational costs and organizational competitiveness. Whereas upper management's thrust was on strategic issues, lower and middle management's attention circled around HR and job-related matters including job design, manpower allocation linked to job requirements such as shifts, absenteeism, retention and attrition, performance appraisals, employee motivation and managing teams.

While opportunities were perceived as exceeding threats thereby resulting in a positive outlook for the future of the ITES–BPO industry, the opportunities highlighted by the managers included high growth potential, new business processes and new client partnerships.

Threats included competition from other countries and from captive ITES–BPO centres as well as increasing costs and client demands (Mehta et al., 2006).

Nonetheless, managers in general seem to be struggling with the problem of attrition. McMillin (2006) highlights that turnover rates continue to be high, in spite of numerous employee benefits such as mentoring and leadership programmes, insurance facilities, loan schemes, educational subsidies, health improvement programmes and recreational opportunities.

The high level of turnover imposes high costs of recruitment and screening on call centres, and managers find themselves in a perpetual search for additional agents. Managers estimated that the costs to recruit, screen and train each new employee averaged over Rs 26,000. These costs do not take into account the lost productivity of new employees. As indicated above, managers of international facing call centres reported that it takes over three months for an agent to become proficient in call centre work. Yet if turnover rates average 30 per cent annually, then average agents are quitting their job at just about the time they become proficient at it (Batt et al., 2005a).

There were several solutions suggested to overcome this impasse. One way to improve the employment stability and benefit from the skills of experienced employees is to offer promotional opportunities to employees. The second approach is to have employees handle more complex calls and complaints from irate customers or to designate them as coaches or on-the-job trainers, pairing them with new employees. A third solution is to use skill-based routing systems to create tiers of jobs, with increasing levels of complexity. A fourth measure is to offer them opportunities for promotions outside the call centre but inside the larger organization, in exchange for serving as a CSR for a minimum period of time. Managers reported that they promote about 15 per cent of their employees to higher positions in the organization. International facing call centres reported promoting 17 per cent of their employees to higher position while domestic call centres reported promotion rates of 11 per cent. Beyond the call centre, however, only about 1 per cent of employees are promoted to higher positions in the larger organization (Batt et al., 2005a).

Budhwar et al. (2006) conclude that while Indian call centres have well-established internal labour markets for recruitment, selection, training and compensation, they are less developed regarding employee career planning, retention and development, thereby defeating the very mandate of internal labour markets. Indeed, attention to employee career planning, retention and development could be critical in stymying attrition.

This book furthers our understanding of the work experiences of Indian call centre agents employed in international facing call centres via an empirical inquiry guided by qualitative research methods.

3

The Research Process

Qualitative research methods trace their intellectual roots to post-positivist epistemology (Schwandt, 1997). Subscribing to positions such as *verstehen*, interpretive sociology, phenomenology and symbolic interactionism, post-positivists reject the imitation of the natural scientist's procedures and advocate greater attention to subjective experiences and feelings (Bryman, 1988). They accept that empirical observations are important but reject the idea that these sense experiences and reason can provide an immutable foundation for knowledge claims (Schwandt, 1997). Instead, the focus is on the interpretation of social phenomena from the point of view of the meanings being employed by the people studied (Bryman and Burgess, 1999). In order to do this, qualitative methods are employed since they involve an interpretive, naturalistic approach to the problem. This means that qualitative researchers study things in their natural setting, attempting to make sense of or interpret phenomena in terms of the meanings people bring to them (Denzin and Lincoln, 1994). Through this process, the researcher builds a holistic and complex picture of the problematic (Creswell, 1998).

Qualitative methods provide well-grounded, rich and contextualized descriptions and explanations of experiences and processes. They allow for the preservation of complexity and chronology as well as the assessment of causality. Serendipitous findings and new theoretical paradigms are likely to emerge (Miles and Huberman, 1994), which can be further studied and developed. Another significant purpose is to challenge the status quo and identify new paradigms or directions of inquiry (Morse, 1991).

Qualitative research includes a variety of traditions, each of which is characterized by a distinct research process. By and large, these strategies have emerged from diverse disciplinary perspectives and often have sub-specialities of their own. Moreover, they are often known by different names, giving rise to a sense of confusion about the choice of approaches available. Creswell (1998), after a careful study of numerous classifications of qualitative methods, concluded that despite the varying labels there are essentially five strategies, namely, biographies, grounded theory, phenomenology, ethnography and case studies. Table 3.1 summarizes the salient features of each approach.

Research Strategy

The attempt to look at the work experiences of call centre agents as lived experience calls into play the phenomenological tradition (Creswell, 1998). Phenomenology derives from the Greek word 'phenomenon' which means to show itself, to put into light or to manifest something that can become visible in itself (Heidegger in Ray, 1994). According to Bishop and Scudder (1991: 5), 'phenomenology attempts to disclose the essential meaning of human endeavours.' Phenomenology includes a variety of distinctive yet related schools that are concerned with philosophy and method (Ray, 1994). Two key thinkers here are Husserl and Heidegger (Cohen and Omery, 1994). Husserl's eidetic–transcendental phenomenology is epistemologic and emphasizes a return to reflective intuition to describe and clarify experience as it is lived and constituted into consciousness (Ray, 1994). Here, it is believed that there are essential structures to any human experience and when these structures are apprehended in consciousness, they take on a meaning that is the truth of that experience for the participants. Methodologically, then, to describe the meaning of an experience from the perspective of those who have had the experience, researchers bracket their presuppositions (epoch), reflect on the experiences described and intuit or describe the essential structures of the experiences under study (Cohen and Omery, 1994). Heidegger's hermeneutic–interpretive approach is ontologic, a way of being in the socio-historical world where the fundamental dimension of all human consciousness is historical and socio-cultural, and is expressed through

TABLE 3.1 Dimensions for Comparing Five Research Traditions in Qualitative Research

Dimension	Biography	Phenomenology	Grounded Theory	Ethnography	Case Study
Focus	Exploring the life of an individual	Understanding the essence of experiences about a phenomenon	Developing a theory grounded in data from the field	Describing and interpreting a cultural and social group	Developing an in-depth analysis of a single case or multiple cases
Discipline origin	Anthropology, Literature, History, Psychology, Sociology	Philosophy, Sociology, Psychology	Sociology	Cultural anthropology, Sociology	Political science, Sociology, Evaluation, Urban studies, other social sciences
Data collection	Primarily interviews and documents	Long interviews with up to 10 people	Interviews with 20–30 individuals to 'saturate' categories and detail a theory	Primarily observations and interviews with additional artefacts during extended time in the field (for example, six months to a year)	Multiple sources—documents, archival records, interviews, observations, physical artefacts
Data analysis	Stories, Epiphanies, Historical content	Statements, Meanings, Meaning themes, General description of the experience	Open coding, Axial coding, Selective coding, Conditional matrix	Description. Analysis. Interpretation	Description, Themes, Assertions
Narrative form	Detailed picture of an individual's life	Description of the 'essence' of the experience	Theory or theoretical model	Description of the cultural behaviour of a group or an individual	In-depth study of a 'case' or 'cases'

Source: Creswell, 1998: 65.

language (Ray, 1994). As a research method, this approach rests on the ontological thesis that lived experience is itself essentially an interpretive process (Cohen and Omery, 1994) within which presuppositions are not to be eliminated or suspended but constitute the possibility of meaning (Ray, 1994). The phenomenological task is one of explicit ontological self-interpretation (Burch, 1989). It is not just watching the phenomena forming themselves into consciousness, but an act of interpretation involving perception whereby sense is brought from historical horizons and contextual factors to crystallize into a gestalt, whose meaning can be fully interpreted only through its history and through its relatedness to things in the world which precede, and always transcend, meaning (Langan, 1970; Spiegelberg, 1982).

Hermeneutic phenomenology is indisputably more ambitious than eidetic phenomenology, going beyond the meaning of what is immediately and directly manifest to our intuiting, analysing and describing, to uncover hidden meanings through the use of the ordinary and the everyday which embody clues for meanings that are usually not explicit (Cohen and Omery, 1994).

Combining the goals of the Husserlian and Heideggerian schools is Dutch phenomenology, whose use in research has been vividly described by van Manen (Cohen and Omery, 1994). Van Manen (1998), whose hermeneutic phenomenological approach was adopted in the present study, portrays the methodical structure of phenomenology as a dynamic interplay between six research activities. According to him, the researcher turns to a phenomenon which seriously interests him/her and commits him/her to this abiding concern. The single-mindedness of purpose results in full thinking and deep questioning, so that we can understand life wholly. The experience is investigated as it is lived rather than as it is conceptualized. In other words, the attempt is to renew contact with the original experience and to become full of it. The researcher then reflects on the essential themes that characterize the phenomenon. A true reflection on lived experience is a thoughtful, reflective grasping of what it is that renders this experience special. The fourth activity is describing the experience and its essence through the art of writing and rewriting. Language and thought need to be applied to lived experience such that a precise depiction is made. In order to achieve all of this, the researcher needs to maintain a strong orientation to the fundamental question so as to maintain direction and to come out with valid findings. He/she also needs to balance the research context by considering parts and wholes, that is, one needs to constantly measure the overall design of the study against the significance that the parts must play in the total structure.

Method

In the phenomenological study, the world of lived experience is both the source and object of research. The point here is to borrow from others' experiences and their reflections on their experiences in order to arrive at a better understanding of the meaning of an aspect of human experience. Though phenomenological studies rely on traditional data collection techniques such as interviews, written responses, observations, etc., the emphasis is not just on reporting subjective experiences of participants, but on asking what makes the phenomenon under study an essentially human one (van Manen, 1998).

Following van Manen's (1998) approach, the conversational interview was used to explore and gather experiential narrative material that would serve as a resource for developing a richer and deeper understanding of the experience being studied. Interviews are preferred to protocol writing because the latter forces the person into a more reflective attitude which may make it difficult to stay close to an experience as it is immediately lived (van Manen, 1998).

Keeping in mind the difficulties of direction that emerge in unstructured interviews, the process was disciplined by focusing on the fundamental question that prompted the research, in keeping with van Manen's (1998) idea that researcher should stay as close to the experience as it is lived. That is, though the interview was unstructured, the researchers carefully considered its purpose at the outset and let this consideration shadow the process so that direction was never lost. Confusion on the part of the researcher clouds the interview, resulting in material that is either too little or too shallow or too long, irrelevant and unmanageable. Yet the clarity of the research question did not preclude exploring issues that emerged during the interview, since the researchers were aware that they could generate important insights into the phenomenon under study.

Though such a data gathering procedure has no scope for ready-made questions, van Manen's (1998) idea of starting with broad cues was followed. As with his observation, here too the researchers noted that these cues stimulated a process of storytelling in the participants. Since a single broad query can yield rich information on an experience, its contexts, its actors, its dynamics, nuances and consequences, its accompanying emotions and interpretations, storytelling usually proceeded without too many questions. Where responses were limited or unclear, probes were used to capture lived experience in depth and completeness. While each response was explored to the fullest, direction in the data gathering was incorporated through the use of cues.

Data Collection

While the study this book is based on forms part of a larger inquiry on employee work experiences in the Indian ITES–BPO sector, undertaken in Mumbai and Bangalore, the book presents the lived experience of international facing call centre agents included in our research.

As is the case with the phenomenological tradition, participants must be those who have experienced the phenomenon, and hence we sought to include call centre agents in our study. With organizations being unwilling to permit us access to their employees or the operations floor (only one inbound Indian third-party call centre in Mumbai gave us access and this happened through personal contacts), we had to resort to snowball sampling for the entire study. We began our initial data collection by relying on informal contacts such as our former students and our social network as well as on the office bearers of the IT Professionals' Forum (ITPF), Centre for BPO Professionals (CBPOP) and UNITES Professionals (Union for ITES Professionals; henceforth also termed as UNITES) (See Chapter 5 for a discussion of ITPF, CBPOP and UNITES)—all these people put us in touch with call centre agents and we relied on snowballing to complete our sample. The use of the mobile phone helped us a lot as we would contact potential respondents via phone and then fix up interviews at places of mutual convenience which were generally restaurants/eating places.

Essentially, during our initial contact with potential participants, we would introduce ourselves and describe our research mandate.

Questions posed by potential participants would be answered. Based on this discussion, once they agreed to participate, a time and a place for the interview were fixed as per mutual convenience. At the time of meeting, researcher details were once again shared along with information about the purpose and scope of the study as well as emphasis on voluntary participation and confidentiality. As mentioned earlier, most interviews were conducted in restaurants/eating places, with a few being held at the ITPF, CBPOP and UNITES offices or at participants' homes.

All interviews were conducted in English. While some interviews were conducted jointly by both the researchers talking to a single participant, there were instances of both the researchers simultaneously interviewing two participants as well as of one researcher interviewing either one or more participants at the same time. All interviews were recorded on audio-cassette with the permission of the participant. No participant objected to the use of the recorder once its advantage of accuracy was spelt out to them, and its presence did not appear to hinder their responses. During the interview, observations about the participants were made and written up after the session ended. Data recorded on the audio-cassette were later transcribed by the research staff.

At least two interview sessions per participant were desired. This would not only facilitate holistic and in-depth exploration of participants' experiences but also allow for initial analysis and follow-up of issues emerging in the first session. Though the preference for two interview sessions was told to the participants during the rapport building process, this did not work out due to various constraints faced by participants. Hence, just one interview session was conducted per participant.

Looking back, we realize that we had contacted a very large pool of potential participants in both Bangalore and Mumbai; however, not everyone agreed to participate and we had interesting experiences on this front. For example, some people agreed to do the interview but would not show up at the appointed place or time. Others would agree initially and refuse later. There were those who would agree initially and later not pick up their phones to further the interaction. Among those we contacted were those who expressed interest in participating but were unable to actually come for an interview due to family responsibilities, work-related travel, etc. These individuals asked about the possibility of phone interviews but we did not accede to this request due to methodological considerations. A few asked us to come through their employers, an avenue that we could not pursue successfully due to reluctance on the part of organizations. We also came across people who flatly refused either due to lack of time, lack of interest, fear of strangers or fear of being reprimanded by their employers.

Other interesting experiences during data collection included the mismatch between our timings and those of call centre agents. Since many of them worked during the night and slept during the day, it was difficult to know when to call them and we could interview them only on weekly holidays when they were free. Quite often weekly holidays were the only time they had for themselves, their families and their personal life and hence they made a special effort to meet us.

In Mumbai, while we found an absence of technical call centres, we observed the presence of domestic call centres and made a concerted effort to include participants from such firms in the study.

Study Participants

While our final sample from both Mumbai and Bangalore comprised 85 call centre agents including 19 Bangalore-based agents who worked in technical call centres and seven Mumbai-based agents who worked in domestic call centres, these latter two groups' experiences are not included within the purview of this book (See D'Cruz and Noronha, 2007, for details about agents' experiences in technical call centres). Of the 59 international facing call centre agents whose experiences are presented in this book, 34 were from Mumbai and 25 were based in Bangalore. Thirty-nine worked in inbound processes, 12 in outbound processes and eight in both inbound and outbound processes (Table 3.2). While there were 29 women and 30 men (Table 3.3) whose ages ranged from 20 to 55 years, the largest number of participants were in the 22 to 25 years age group (Table 3.4). Forty participants were unmarried (Table 3.5) and forty were graduates (Table 3.6). The mean monthly salary of participants was approximately Rs 12,900, based on a range of Rs 8,000 to Rs 25,000 (Table 3.7). All the participants were employed by either MNC captive, MNC third-party or Indian

TABLE 3.2 Location of Participants

	Inbound	Outbound	Inbound and Outbound	Total
Bangalore	14	5	6	25
Mumbai	25	7	2	34
Total	39	12	8	59

TABLE 3.3 Gender of Participants

	Male	Female	Total
Bangalore	16	9	25
Mumbai	14	20	34
Total	30	29	59

TABLE 3.4 Age of Participants (in years)

	18–21	22–25	26–29	30+	Not Known	Total
Bangalore	2	16	3	3	1	25
Mumbai	4	12	4	9	5	34
Total	6	28	7	12	6	59

TABLE 3.5 Marital Status of Participants

	Unmarried	Married	Separated	Widowed	Not Known	Total
Bangalore	20	4	1	0	0	25
Mumbai	20	12	0	0	2	34
Total	40	16	1	0	2	59

TABLE 3.6 Educational Level of Participants

	12th Grade or Less	Undergraduate	Graduate	Postgraduate	Not Known	Total
Bangalore	0	5	19	1	0	25
Mumbai	0	9	21	0	4	34
Total	0	14	40	1	4	59

TABLE 3.7 Monthly Salary of Participants (in Indian Rupees)

	Range	Average	Did not Disclose	Not Known
Bangalore	8,000 to 25,000	13,300 approximately	1	2
Mumbai	8,000 to 23,000	12,500 approximately	–	6

Note: Overall mean = Rs 12,900 approximately per month.

third-party organizations and served overseas clients and customers. None of the participants were members of any unions.

Data Analysis

The treatment and analysis of data followed van Manen (1998). The purpose of phenomenological reflection is to grasp the essential meaning of something. The insight into the essence of a phenomenon involves a process of reflectively appropriately clarifying and making explicit the structure of meaning of the lived experience. Meaning is multi-dimensional and multi-layered, and can be best communicated through organized narrative or text. To do human science research is to be involved in the crafting of a text which describes the phenomenon in terms of themes (van Manen, 1998).

In defining themes, van Manen (1998) states that themes touch at the core of the notion we are trying to understand, helping us to make sense. Since they may not always completely unlock the enigmatic aspects of the experience, related sub-themes, capturing details and nuances may be required to provide a comprehensive picture. The notion of theme implies making something of a lived experience by interpreting its meaning through a process of insightful invention, discovery or disclosure. Thematic analysis refers to the process of recovering the themes that are embodied or dramatized in the evolving meanings and imagery of the text.

Themes may be isolated through three approaches (van Manen, 1998):

1. Holistic or sententious approach where we attend to the text as a whole and capture its fundamental meaning.
2. Selective or highlighting approach where we repeatedly read/listen to the text and examine the meaning of statements which are particularly revealing.
3. Detailed or line-by-line approach where we study every sentence or sentence cluster to determine what it says about the experience.

In the present study, the attempt to isolate themes involved the first two approaches. Transcripts and field notes were read several times in order to gain a sense of the overall experience of the participant. Through the holistic approach, the researcher tried to develop an idea of what it meant for a person to live the experience. Following the identification of the essential theme, selective reading was undertaken where significant statements, related to and illustrating the various dimensions of the essential theme, were identified and demarcated. These were read and reread to formulate conceptual meanings and explore essential qualities of described experiences, and themes were identified in the process. As the themes emerged, components of each participant's statements relevant for each meaning unit were highlighted. Redundancies in the units were eliminated and relevant statements were clustered. The essence of agents' experiences was embodied in the core theme of being professional. Chapter 4 puts forward the core theme and its constituents via a text that captures lived experience in its completeness.

We attempted to deepen our understanding of the core theme and its constituents in two ways. First, we looked at the notion of professionalism as delineated by participants against the concept of professionalism as discussed by the taxonomic and power approaches within the sociology of the professions. This analysis is presented in Chapter 6. Second, we undertook further research with two other groups, that is, labour activists and trade unionists active in the Indian ITES–BPO sector and managers employed in call centre organizations in Bangalore and Mumbai.

Data collected from the trade unionists and labour activists, presented in Chapter 5, threw light on how the union movement strategizes to reinvent itself to organize effectively, taking into account the professional orientation of call centre agents. Data were gathered via individual in-depth interviews with Union Network International–Asia Pacific Regional Office (UNI–APRO), ITPF, CBPOP and UNITES office bearers, participation at union meetings and perusal of documents and web pages. Both individual interviews and union meetings were audio recorded with prior permission and were transcribed. Data were analyzed to provide a chronological account of the collectivist movement in the ITES–BPO sector and to highlight and capture emergent thematic areas. Miles and Huberman's (1994) data analysis techniques facilitated this process. That is, through the use of various tools such as charts, matrices, event lists, causal networks and memos (Miles and

Huberman, 1994), the researchers identified themes, categories and patterns emerging from the data. Linkages between themes, patterns and categories were examined, and interpretations were made (Patton, 1990). Further, those themes, patterns and categories and their linkages, within and across participants, that held together in a meaningful yet distinct way, were subsumed under major themes. Interpretations based on this level of analysis were made.

In-depth interviews were conducted with 40 call centre managers in Bangalore and Mumbai (7 women and 33 men, 27 from Bangalore and 13 from Mumbai, all employed with MNC captive/MNC third party/ Indian third party call centre organizations), examining employee experiences, work conditions, organizational culture and managerial practices. Managers were identified via snowball sampling through ITPF/CBPOP/UNITES office bearers, personal contacts and contacts of agents who participated in the study. Transcripts, derived from the interview data (that were audio recorded with permission), were analyzed using Miles and Huberman's (1994) techniques, and major themes were developed. That is, through the use of various tools such as charts, matrices, event lists, causal networks and memos (Miles and Huberman, 1994), the researchers identified themes, categories and patterns emerging from the data. Linkages between themes, patterns and categories were examined, and interpretations were made (Patton, 1990). Further, those themes, patterns and categories and their linkages, within and across participants, that held together in a meaningful yet distinct way, were subsumed under major themes. Interpretations based on this level of analysis were made. Managerial views, as described in Chapter 6, while acknowledging call centre organizations' reliance on the notion of professionalism, pointed out contradictions between employers' conceptualization of professionalism as communicated to employees and the actual operationalization of professionalism within the organization.

It is relevant to point out that participants' quotes are included in Chapters 4, 5 and 6 to illustrate the various themes.

Methodological rigour in the study was maintained through prolonged engagement (Lincoln and Guba, 1985), sources and investigators triangulation (Lincoln and Guba, 1999) and consensual validation (Lincoln and Guba, 1999). Prolonged engagement led the researchers to spend a lot of time in the field to understand its subtleties and nuances. In relation to the use of interviews, particular importance was given to rapport building with the participants—it was opined that making the participants feel comfortable and establishing their trust would play a critical role in helping them to share their stories. During the course of the interviews, the researchers used probes and cross-checks to further their understanding of participants' narratives. Sources triangulation strengthened the robustness of the study since a deeper perspective covering several dimensions of the problematic could be simultaneously captured. Investigators triangulation ensured that each researcher kept the other one 'honest' (Lincoln and Guba, 1999: 412), adding to the credibility of the findings. Immersion in the data during the process of analysis helped the researchers gain insight into participant experiences and perspectives and ensure the rigour of the findings.

van Manen (1998) proposes formal or informal hermeneutic conversations with other researchers on core themes and themes in order to generate deeper insights. Themes are examined, articulated, reinterpreted, added, omitted and reformulated. The attempt is to derive a common orientation to the experience and to help the researcher see limits in his/her present vision and to transcend them. A collaborative rather than competitive stance is indispensable here. Realizing the significance of this process for incorporating methodological rigor in the research, the researchers followed it in all the data analysis phases. Core themes, major themes, themes, emerging conceptual categories and patterns were discussed and critiqued with research colleagues and experts in qualitative research. Based on the emerging discourse, reformulations were made till a consensual validation was achieved.

Overall, the study facilitated theoretical generalizability (Strauss and Corbin, 1998; Thompson, 1999), allowing our knowledge of concepts to be informed to a broader theoretical understanding (Thompson, 1999).

4
Professionalism as Lived Experience

The essence of agents' experiences was embodied in the core theme of being professional. The notion of professionalism embraced agents' identity, altering their self-concept and enhancing their self-esteem. According to agents, professionals possess superior cognitive abilities, advanced qualifications and a sense of responsibility and commitment to work. They prioritize work over personal needs and pleasure, behaving in a dignified and restrained manner and performing optimally and rationally while on the job. Professionals comply with job and organizational requirements, absorbing emergent strain. Under such circumstances, not only do agents perceive gains accruing from their job as consistent with the notion of professionalism but also transactional psychological contracts of employment as means of discipline are similarly justified. Though resistance is displayed by some agents a few times, this is described as a temporary outlet to ease job-related strain, coexisting with professional identity—it is not an indicator of anti-work or anti-employer sentiment. Indeed, agents' professional identity precludes engagement with collectivization attemts which are seen both as inconsistent with the essential features of professionalism and as redundant in instances where employers protect employee interests.

Through agents' narratives, the context surrounding their professional identity came out vividly. Organizations cultivated the notion of professionalism in employees through induction training, on-going socialization, performance evaluation mechanisms and other elements of organizational design, with a view to gain their compliance and commitment to the realization of the organization's agenda. That professional identity is greatly valued as a symbol of social status and upward mobility in the Indian context facilitated the process (see Chapter 5). Indeed, professional identity allowed agents to accept task and organizational demands in spite of the strain they engendered. Material artefacts and organizational processes were cited as proof of organization's espousal of professionalism. Though, in reality, organizations did not fully deliver on their claims relating to the latter (see Chapter 6), professed commitment to employee well-being, rooted in the notion of professionalism, served organizational interests in maintaining a conducive intra-organizational and extra-organizational environment that allowed business to flourish. This chapter presents the themes that make up the core theme.

It is relevant to point out at this juncture that agents' lived experience demonstrates contemporary employer organizations' growing reliance on the appeal of professionalism (Evetts, 2003 and 2006; Fournier, 1999) as a means of identity regulation and socio-ideological control in order to achieve the organizational agenda (see Chapter 7 for a discussion).

Justifying Organizational Requirements, Task-related Demands and Technobureaucratic Controls

Agents' professional identity coloured their perceptions of and responses to organizational and job demands. Being employed by international facing call centres, agents served overseas clients and customers. That is, whether the firm they were employed with was MNC captive, MNC third-party or Indian third-party, the clients were based either in the USA, Canada, UK or Australia and had a formalized relationship (also known as a service level agreement [SLA]), either temporal or project-based, with participants' employer organizations (the offshored Indian/India-based service providers) to deliver stipulated services to their customers who were also located overseas. The SLA between the client and the employer organization laid down the process and outcome requirements of the particular service, the fulfilment of which was critical to the continuity and/or renewal of the contractual relationship between the two parties. With competitive advantage being the key focus, employer organizations diligently implemented client expectations and this set the work context for participants.

Apart from having to work in shifts and sometimes adopt accents and pseudonyms and conceal their geographical location to suit their foreign customers, participants had to meet SLA requirements that encompassed various aspects of task performance such as targets, average handling time (AHT) of the call, call wrap-up time, call waiting time, call abandonment rates, call opening and closing, customer interaction including sensitivity, politeness, warmth, understanding customer needs and handling irate customers, adherence to the script, fluency in the English language, understanding of the process, use of a neutral accent, maintenance of prescribed procedures including assistance offered and information provided, accuracy of documentation, and other parameters specified by the client; all of which were monitored essentially through technology-based mechanisms. Technobureaucratic measures, on the lines of those outlined by McPhail (2002), thus served as important controls. Further, participants included in this book were employed by call centres that combined mass production and customer orientation, resembling the mass customized model of Batt and Moynihan (2002) and Frenkel et al. (1998). Hence, while participants' jobs entailed little complexity, variety and autonomy, completion of high volumes and provision of good quality service proceeded concomitantly. Participants worked in teams, headed by a TL. Performance, which was linked to the award of incentives over and above salary and to promotion opportunities, was evaluated at individual and team levels.

Failure to meet employer organizations' expectations whether in matters of job performance, task-related requirements or general workplace etiquette, resulted in punishments. While punishments ranged from warnings, retraining and suspension to termination and dismissal, the degree of punishment awarded depended on the nature and frequency of the offence. With termination and dismissal being used even in cases of confirmed employees, the primacy of transactional psychological contracts (Rousseau, 1990) was evident. As Ramesh (2004) says, a confirmation letter means nothing—agents enjoy titular status and can be terminated any time without notice.

Adherence to job and organizational demands as well as discipline at and priority towards work were constantly emphasized, linked to the notion of professionalism. That is, employer organizations cultivated the notion of professionalism in their agents in order to gain the latter's compliance and commitment to the realization of organizational goals. It was thus not surprising that agents, while acknowledging the nature and requirements of their jobs, saw nothing amiss in their work situation, maintaining that the acceptance and fulfilment of such job-related demands formed an integral part of a professional's life. Clearly, agents' professional sense of self worked in a pervasive manner, disciplining them on the job and ensuring that they behaved objectively and rationally and performed optimally.

> We have to stick to what we have to do. Don't go out of it, unless we are asked. Do your best, that's it. You will be recognized. Be in good terms with your seniors. Don't be harsh in the team. That is professional.[1]

Participant narratives highlighted stringent work conditions including the hours of work, the pace of work, quality and quantity parameters, monitoring and feedback as well as emphasis on rules and etiquette. In order to meet client requirements, employer organizations created 8–9 hour shifts with two 15-minute breaks and one 30-minute break, and 5-day work weeks. Agents were required to report half an hour before their assigned shift for team meetings. During these meetings, TLs indicated daily requirements, proposed updates, provided individual and team feedback and attempted to energize the team besides checking the functioning of work-related equipment and technology. Participants' adherence to shift timings was recorded via log in and log out data. Participants mentioned how such strict observation of time meant that they could not log out of their systems or leave their seats even to go to the restroom (if it was an emergency, they had to seek permission from the TL to do so). During phases when call volumes were high or targets were not being met, agents were made to stretch such that they had to forfeit or shorten breaks and/or work beyond shift hours or on weekly/public holidays. It is relevant to

---

[1] Participant quotes are included in this chapter to illustrate the various themes. For reasons of confidentiality, participants have not been identified individually.

mention that the public holidays (both national holidays and festivals) observed were in accordance with those of the customer group being served and not Indian holidays. Moreover, quite often, agents received no overtime for the extra work put in. Further, for those aspiring to move up the organizational hierarchy initially to become TLs and later managers, additional initiatives beyond the stipulated job description requirements (such as helping their TL in call escalation, preparing reports or managing the floor in the TL's absence) were undertaken in order to increase one's visibility and create a favourable impression. This extended work time and increased job demands.

> Even though they say 9 hours of work, it is never 9 hours. You put in 10 hours, 12 hours, etc. After 9 hours of work, I have to meet my superiors, submit reports and all. So it will all come to 12 hours of work. When I reach home 3 hours after work, there won't be any time for other things. I was a customer support executive only on paper. They give you a team of 8 and you have to carry out all the responsibilities of a TL. So at the end of the day, I will be doing the work of a TL, team coach (TC) and all. It was good for sometime. But it was too much of workload. You have to do escalations during the shift hours. After 9 hours of shift work, you have to make team reports, report absenteeism and quality, etc. Everyday, it was a 12 hours job. And I did it. Everyone does it. All the TLs do it. It will help you in some way. It is important to do this to move up, people see you positively.

Whereas inbound call centre agents had to take the maximum number of calls possible in a shift, for outbound call centre agents, targets were fixed in terms of completion of a specific number of units pertaining to the particular process being performed. In the latter case, for instance, if the agent was engaged in a collections process, he/she had to finish a specific number of collections per shift. Similarly, telemarketing agents had to complete a minimum number of sales per shift. Agents were always encouraged to achieve beyond their specified targets and being able to do so was adjudged an indicator of their level of professionalism. Undoubtedly, achieving beyond specific targets augmented their incentives and added to their visibility and opportunities for growth.

As pointed out in the preceding paragraphs, for telemarketing agents, the hallmark of competence was the ability to convert calls into sales and to meet/surpass targets. Indeed, telemarketing agents were constantly reminded by their TLs and other superiors that their worth lay in generating revenue for the organization. The onus was thus placed upon the agent to create customer interest in, and then sell, a particular product or service. While being unable to see the customer physically put agents at a disadvantage when proposing a sale, experience with emotional labour skills helped them to decipher the mood of the customer before they attempted to pitch for a sale. Telemarketing agents admitted that they did not mind being flirted with or being screamed at by the customers if they could strike a deal. In keeping with Brannan (2005), then, there were instances where agent sexuality was mobilized on behalf of the organization in order to effect smoother interactions. Converting a call into a sale translated into a tremendous sense of achievement and satisfaction, besides ensuring continuity with the organization and increase in salary as a bonus. Those failing to meet targets or put in the required log-in hours were asked to work on holidays. When participants were able to make sales after an unsuccessful spell, their relief was palpable. Inability to perform resulted in the employee being sent for retraining which essentially meant notice before dismissal.

> Once you give your numbers, your job is done...Getting the sales is the most important thing and they keep track of it throughout the shift—if you don't get a sale, then people will come and stand behind you saying that you didn't get a sale. Every one hour or so, they will call and ask, 'How many sales you made?'. You feel different when you didn't make a sale. When others have made four sales and you made none, you feel odd, you feel very depressed. Because they will come and straight away compare, 'He is a normal person like you getting a sale, then why can't you?'

> Everyday, you have to make sales. So if you don't achieve the sale, they will mark you. If I cannot achieve the target for 3–4 days, they will call and ask, 'What are your problems—any personal or family problems—how can we solve them?' If we do not perform, they will say, 'Man, you are not generating any revenue for the company. So still you want us to give you time or are you going?' They will ask straight away.

Participant narratives alluded to numerous monitoring and surveillance mechanisms employed by call centre organizations. Apart from technology-based systems directly related to task performance (as described in the following paragraphs), agents spoke about the presence of security personnel who conducted random security checks of their person and their belongings prior to them entering their offices. Lockers were provided by the employer within the office premises but outside the call floor for agents to store their belongings during the shift. Agents were not permitted to carry anything (including a piece of paper, a purse, a mobile phone, water/eatables) into or out from the call floor, and security personnel manning the electronically operated doors at the entrance/exit of the call floor ensured that they complied. All materials required for task performance were provided inside the call floor, as also drinking water and sometimes tea and coffee. Such practices were described as part of client specifications to maximize the security of the process and the protection of customers' interests.

Technology dominated participants' work context and work experience. Participants worked in technologically-driven environments equivalent to those in developed countries. As pointed out earlier by Taylor and Bain (2005), our participants too worked with ACD systems plugged into the same turrets found on workstations abroad through which calls were distributed and queue numbers and waiting times were displayed. Agents navigated familiar screens and menus, entering data on globally-branded computers (Taylor and Bain, 2005). With ACD technology systematizing control and possessing the power to push and pace work (Callaghan and Thompson, 2001), management could set and measure daily output without the need for constant and direct control while agents experienced restricted autonomy (van den Broek, 2004). Predictive dialling in outbound centres ensured that customer calls were diverted automatically to agents who were currently not engaged on another call. Not surprisingly, then, on days when the call flow was very high, agents took back-to-back calls. During such times, agents enjoyed neither breathing space nor breaks.

> Taking calls is stressful. Taking calls for 8 hours continuously in a day—you finish a call and you will get next. You keep on working like this for one year and you will be so fed up of taking calls. So one gets stressed out.

Agents from inbound centres recounted being confronted with prominent digital displays which emphasize the number of stacked calls waiting to be answered. Taylor and Bain (1999) describe such a situation as 'an assembly-line in the head' which precipitates perennial pressure in agents, stemming from the knowledge that the completion of the current call signifies the onset of the next one in a never-ending queue.

In addition to targets, agents' work is regulated by numerous quality and quantity parameters, and technology facilitates their monitoring and measurement. The ACD system throws up a range of statistics, and various 'hard' or quantitative measures are collected routinely and regularly for each call centre agent individually and for his/her work team collectively. These include call-waiting time, average call handling time (AHT), call wrap-up time and call abandonment rates (Kinnie et al., 2000). Call barging (where TLs, quality analysts and other superiors—and in some cases, even clients—listen in simultaneously but remotely on live calls to evaluate agents' performance) and sidejacking (where TLs, quality analysts and other superiors physically sit next to the agent and listen and evaluate his/her call) also form part of performance management. In addition, since all calls are recorded and stored in archives, calls can be retrieved at any time and analyzed for the purpose of evaluation and appraisal. It was not uncommon for recorded calls to be randomly pulled out by analysts in the quality department and examined in terms of call opening and closing, customer interaction including sensitivity, politeness, warmth, understanding customer needs and handling irate customers, adherence to the script, fluency in the English language, understanding of the product/service/process, use of a neutral accent, maintenance of prescribed procedures including assistance offered and information provided, accuracy of documentation, and other parameters specified by the client. Recording of calls ensured that agents in telemarketing call centres do not provide wrong information or make false promises in order to fulfil their sales targets and augment their earnings.

The employment of call centre technology as a monitoring and measurement device did not spell the end of human supervision, as stated by Taylor and Bain (1999). TLs, stationed at a central point on the call floor, were always in a position to overlook the operations and keep an eye on the agents, seconding Ramesh's (2004) observation, in addition to having a master screen on their computers which tracked and highlighted in real time the on-going work of each individual agent in the team.

Participants' initial reactions to the intensive and constant monitoring and surveillance were mixed. On one hand, it unnerved them. Reports of self-consciousness and nervousness were common. On the other hand, they believed that not only were such measures part of client requirements specified in the SLAs and hence an unavoidable part of the work context but also that the feedback they received from such measures facilitated their performance and ensured their career progress. As professionals, they had to put organizational interests and work demands above their personal discomfort. At the same time, task performance could be scaled up to higher levels of professionalism via the feedback received.

Some agents opined that being able to cope with the discomfort of being monitored prepared them to deal with the bigger challenge of handling irate customers.

> There is certainly going to be stress and pressure if someone is directly side-jacking you, but if you are not ready for these things, then how will one handle irate customers? How would you handle the pressure if you don't know how to react to these situations? Irate customers are definitely more stressful than barging. Barging definitely helps the agent to improve his confidence level. Once your confidence is up, you can do anything, you can converse, you can take calls, achieve targets and so on.

Over time, participants grew accustomed to being monitored and then only the latter set of views prevailed. Moreover, participants also acknowledged that monitoring and surveillance served as means of protecting them from potential customer and/or client allegations, which could sometimes even take the form of lawsuits.

As participants elaborated, feedback emanating from monitoring helped agents to understand their shortcomings, overcome deficiencies and enhance their capacity to handle calls and iron out errors. In other words, feedback had no negative connotation attached to it but was seen as being supportive of the agents' effort, serving as an opportunity to learn from those who had a sound knowledge about the process, to improve oneself and to take advantage of further training and coaching and performance improvement plans, if required.

> When you talk to a customer, they record the call, and later on, they will try to identify where we have gone wrong. On a particular call, the customer

might want to know more about the product—so in our eagerness to explain the features of the product, we may make mistakes or talk about the climate, which is not in keeping with the customer's conditions. That's why they record the calls and play it to us later, in the process pinpointing our mistakes, warning us to never repeat them. That's how you can improve.

There is a quality management team who records and hears your calls and gives feedback. Sometimes, while on the call, they will cut it and talk to you over the phone itself, saying, 'This is the mistake you made. Otherwise, you would have got the sale.'

Feedback was also seen as helpful to distinguish between good performers and average ones, encouraging those with drive and dedication to move up the organization while preventing shirking. In the same vein, poor performers who did not meet expectations in spite of being put on performance improvement plans, received no sympathy. Dismissing them was considered to be an appropriate step.

Job design elements and technobureaucratic controls together contributed to a high stress work environment for agents. In other words, though on the one hand, participants' tasks lacked variety, complexity and autonomy resulting in a routinized monotony, on the other hand, stringent quality and quantity parameters enforced via technology-based monitoring and surveillance ensured that agents met organizational and client expectations. Notwithstanding the intense pressure, rationality, objectivity and optimal performance always took precedence, being described as indicators of professionalism. Emotions, subjectivity and relationships were accorded secondary status.

My TL is very close to me. We are like friends. He is younger to me. He is 21 and I am 23. He was my trainer. When he was a trainer, I was in his batch. When I came to the call floor, he was promoted as a TL, and luckily, he became my TL. We became very close friends. But he was very professional. I have never seen a person who is professional like him. Before we enter the call floor, we have to leave our mobile phones in the locker—if we fail to do so, a fine has to be paid. On one particular day, I carried the phone to the floor. My friend (the TL) caught me and asked me to hand over the phone to him. I told him not to tell anybody about it but he insisted that I hand over the phone to him. When I handed over the phone, he told me to pay the fine. He told me, 'Friendship outside, be professional inside.' I was lucky because I was in his team and I learned many things.

It is relevant to mention that in addition to demands and requirements directly related to task performance, employer organizations laid down general etiquette rules which were strictly maintained. Agents were expected to behave politely, displaying respect towards everyone at the workplace in spite of the informal atmosphere.

> Professionalism means punctuality, doing your job to the best of your ability, the way you dress, the way you move with people…Bringing in personal grudges, favouritism—that is not professionalism.

Apart from being well-groomed and appropriately dressed, agents were expected to conduct themselves in a dignified manner. Participants provided an illustration of the latter by citing the case of workplace romances. They highlighted that public displays of affection, flirtatious behaviour and acts of intimacy between couples were not tolerated during office hours and were treated with warnings and even dismissals. Romantic relationships were part of personal life and did not concern the organization—hence they should not impinge on task performance but should be reserved for non-office hours.

> Once a thing happened…there was a girl and a guy who tried to do something in the office. The boy was chucked out and the girl was sent for training or something.

> The company tells us to be professional. They say, 'You may have your girlfriend working with you. But in the workplace, she is only your colleague.' I deserve to be thrown out if I kiss her on the floor.

Dressing 'provocatively' was seen as both causing a distraction from work and creating an unprofessional atmosphere, and could invite punishment.

> One of the clients has settled down in Bangalore, so they might walk in any time. They say that they want us to be professional, they want to see British influence here. So if you are wearing jeans, they might think that you are a casual kind of guy. But if you are in formals, they will feel that you are a decent guy.

> If you walk into a call centre, it's a professional environment. Strictly, no sleeveless tops on the floor. If you come in that, you will be sent home where you have to change and come back. It's because we don't want that slight

feeling to come into people's mind. If a guy comes with an open shirt, we would say, 'Come on, you button up your shirt and never do this again.' So there is a professional atmosphere.

The Primacy of the Customer

Emotional labour remains central to task performance in call centres. Located at the customer-service provider organization/client interface, call centre agents represent the service provider organization/client to customers and hence how they behave during these encounters becomes critical (Ashforth and Humphrey, 1993; Morris and Feldman, 1996). Not surprisingly, then, service provider organizations/clients are increasingly willing to direct and control how employees present themselves to customers (Hochschild, 1983). Agents included in this book described organizational endeavours and related employee training undertaken towards this end. Incorporation of emotional labour requirements into performance measures, especially qualitative parameters, reinforced the position. With customer satisfaction being as important as production levels, employer organizations monitor agent interactions with customers, rewarding those who perform emotional labour as expected and punishing those who do not. This notion of the customer now being fundamental to current management paradigms as a means of analyzing and defining work performance and work relations is dominant in call centres (Du Gay and Salaman, 1992). Participants, viewing the primacy accorded to the customer through the lens of their professional identity, accepted both the gains and demands of emotional labour. According to them, complying with the requirements associated with emotional labour was part of being professional.

Communicating effectively with customers was emphasized. This encompassed clarity and accuracy of communication, adherence to scripts such that providing wrong information and misleading customers was avoided, politeness, cordiality, sensitivity and patience (particularly with irate customers). All this had to be accomplished in a virtual context, concomitant with other process requirements, in real time. In keeping with Belt et al. (1999a), agents had to smile down the phone. Agents were trained to believe that since customers could decipher their moods, the espousal and display of a positive frame of mind was important to induce a similar demeanour in customers, to enhance the perceived quality of the service interaction and to leave behind a favourable impression about the client. To this end, agents were encouraged to empathize with and absorb customer reactions, apologizing to them for any perceived or attributed problem or inconvenience even if it was not their fault. At the same time, maintaining objectivity was emphasized. That is, agents were not allowed to develop personal relationships with customers or display any partiality towards them. Interactions had to be limited to the business at hand. Agents thus had to relate to customers enough to perform effective emotional labour, ensure customer satisfaction and promote client interests while simultaneously meeting other qualitative and quantitative performance criteria. Clearly, as earlier stated by Houlihan (2000) and Korczynski (2002), conflicting role requirements were imposed on agents in terms of the challenge of trying to get closer to the customer while reducing costs, prescribing standards and meeting targets.

> In a call centre, you are forced to finish the call and even if the customer wants to be personal, you cannot be so. You need to tell him, 'Hey! My time limit is going up.' You also have the quality in your mind, AHT and all that stuff. In a call centre, time is the most important factor because, based on the AHT, they analyze you and mark your ratings.

Moreover, agents were trained to set aside their own emotions prior to the shift, in a bid to focus their energies on the task. Being preoccupied with personal affective issues during the shift was described by superiors as interfering with optimal performance and as unprofessional. The ability to remain calm under pressure and to maintain a friendly and tactful attitude while at the same time being psychologically disengaged from the customer, as noted by Rose and Wright (2005), was emphasized. Agents who were seen as being unable to comply with the foregoing requirements were invited to share and work out their problems with TLs and other superiors so that they could eliminate impediments to the performance of emotional labour.

> Your personal and professional selves have to be detached. Only when you are detached, you are able to do well. You go to the office with your problems in your head—obviously, you are not making a good day.

In the very first place, you should keep aside your emotions. Emotions don't play a part here—it's only collections you are coming for. No emotions on the floor. And even if you have emotions, before coming to the floor, you have to leave it. You have had a fight with your Dad or Mom, you have to keep it outside and enter the floor.

When you come to call centers, you become professional. You forget about your emotions and everything. We don't think even what we did in the last call.

For Indian agents working in international facing call centres, training in emotional labour skills went beyond the scope of customer interaction and satisfaction, as described above, to embrace cultural, linguistic and geographical dimensions linked to the lives of their overseas customers. Clients had laid down these latter set of requirements to ensure that customers remained comfortable with and willing to divulge personal information during service interactions, apart from continuing to harbour perceptions of satisfaction over service quality, in spite of migration of services via offshoring and outsourcing (Taylor and Bain, 2005). Through the training, agents not only acquired the requisite skills and abilities but also learnt to accept them as part of the job, being linked to SLAs, process continuity/renewal, organizational success and their own positions. Accordingly, appropriate measurement parameters and related rewards and punishments formed part of agents' evaluation. Not surprisingly, agents viewed these requirements as part of their professional sense of self.

Cultural training included exposure to various facets of customers' society including its geographic location, political boundaries, time zone, climate, history, demographics and way of life. As pointed out previously by Poster (2007) and Taylor and Bain (2005), details about national emblems such as flags, flowers, birds, national anthem, national holidays, festivals, leisure and sporting preferences, currency and slang and colloquialisms were provided. Agents were shown films and/or advised to watch films and television channels such as the British Broadcasting Corporation (BBC), Cable News Network (CNN), National Geographic, Discovery Channel and History Channel in order to deepen their understanding of customers' culture (D'Cruz and Noronha, 2006). Cultural training as well as digital boards, rows of clocks, maps and collages on the walls showing updated details of time, weather, news and other facts and information about customers' location provided on the call floor (Poster, 2007) aided agents in conversing knowledgeably with customers during calls, should the occasion arise.

Linguistic training formed an important component in agents' preparation process. While agents' fluency with English and neutral accents were checked at the time of recruitment, training emphasized the adoption of accents appropriate to and familiarity with local speech such as slang and colloquialisms of the customer group being served. Cowie (2007) speaks of phonetics classes mostly taken up with either mock calls or practice reading passages where the phonetics trainer provided feedback centred around the required pronunciation of individual words. Mastering tongue twisters helped to improve pronunciation in order to challenge Western prejudices about Indians' imperfect speech (Taylor and Bain, 2005). D'Cruz and Noronha (2006) describe how agents were shown movies like 'My Fair Lady' to exemplify spoken English as well as 'Bend It Like Beckham' to contrast the way Indians spoke English with the way the British spoke English. While those who succeeded in mastering the required accent did not face embarrassing customer questions of mother tongue influence (MTI) or of being of Indian origin (D'Cruz and Noronha, 2006), it was difficult for a few agents to acquire a new accent.

> Yes, it was difficult for me because I am from Kerala. There are certain kind of words that we have to pronounce in their way. Here usually we say 'computer', but in UK they say 'compuutter'. They will stress 't'. Initially, the customer did not understand a single word I said. If I were in the customer's position and could not understand what the agent told me, why should I buy the product? Just bang the phone.

Linguistic training served the purpose of facilitating mutual understanding between customers and agents (D'Cruz and Noronha, 2006; Taylor and Bain, 2005), the aim being to refine agents' language such that they could blend in with customers and appear less Indian (Cohen and El-Sawad, 2007). Indeed, agents indicated that they used accents during calls only, confirming Cohen and El-Sawad's (2007) utilitarian approach rather than Mirchandani's (2003b) language imperialism.

Apart from adopting the accent and linguistic mannerisms of the customer group, agents took on pseudonyms and engaged in locational masking. Agents chose Western names as pseudonyms relying either on a list of names given to them by their employer organizations or on their knowledge of famous personalities especially movie or rock stars. Some of them selected names that were clear to hear and easy to pronounce. Others opted for names that started with the same alphabet as that in their original name so that it was easier for them to remember. Indian Christian agents who already had Western names had no need to adopt a pseudonym.

Locational masking, a term coined by Mirchandani (2003b), entails refusal to divulge the geographical base of the offshored call centre and the agent. Non-disclosure agreements between employer organizations and clients do not allow agents to reveal their identity and the location of their call centre, and hence agents are trained to avoid answering such questions from customers. In response to customer queries, agents were trained to say that they were headquartered in the clients' or customers' country. If quizzed further, they either refused to disclose any more information about their location citing security reasons or they would mention that they were located in Asia. Only if the customer persisted or if customer inquiries narrowed down to the specific place from where they were calling, would agents divulge the truth or allow the customer to hang up. In their words:

> They don't want to speak to an Indian. They will ask, 'Where are you located?' We tell them that our head office is at Texas. They insist, 'No, I asked you where you are located.' We then tell them, 'Sorry, due to security reasons, we cannot disclose.' They then say, 'What the crap are you saying? Why should I disclose my personal details to a terrorist country?' They enquire whether we are located in India or Pakistan and compel us to disclose our location. When we say that we are in India, they disconnect the call.

> In most of the call centres, they ask you to use a neutral accent so customers think that we are in the country to which we make the call. We have to disguise and dodge the question 'where you are calling from?'

When customers believed agents' claimed location, it was likely that they could pose further queries about the place. Here too, appropriate cultural training as well as updated information about time, weather, news and other facts and information about the particular location provided on the call floor (Poster, 2007) aided agents in keeping up with any potential questions about their claimed geographical base.

Though agents maintained that cultural and linguistic training, adoption of pseudonyms and locational masking were means of bridging the credibility gap, a seemingly inevitable obstacle in the offshoring process (Cohen and El-Sawad, 2007), a closer examination revealed multiple nuances in their reactions.

Pseudonyms, for instance, served various purposes. Assuming a Western identity was seen as not only helping customers feel more secure in the belief that they were dealing with their fellow countryperson but also as facilitating ease of interaction since customers could relate to a familiar, local name rather than an unfamiliar, Indian name. The latter reason was linked to reducing call AHT and improving performance.

> When you say, 'This is _____ (actual name), calling from _____ (client's name)', the customer responds, 'Who? Can you repeat your name?' or they may ask, 'Are you an Indian?' So the topic moves on to something else—you have to make a sale in a time period. At the end of the day, we are calculating the target issues. So we have to be very quick on calls…so if I say that I am _____ (actual name) then they won't understand it and it will take time.

As the foregoing quote illustrates, it was easier for customers to understand and pronounce agents' assumed names and the latter did not have to waste time spelling out each and every syllable for customers to understand. Employer organizations and clients stood to benefit as targets could be more easily met and costs cut down.

Most agents accepted the need to adopt pseudonyms as part of job requirements. Some of our participants equated the experience with that of being an actor or wearing a mask during work, which was removed or discarded after the shift. Others were happy to assume a Western identity, so much respected and coveted in the Indian context. Participants here indicated that taking on anglicized names made them feel American, British, Canadian or Australian as the case may be, and since they held these societies in great esteem, their self-concept was enhanced.

> When they call me by my professional name, I feel I am a professional, a telemarketer working in an international company, dealing with international guys.

Indeed, so comfortable and pleased were a few agents with the adoption of a pseudonym that they preferred to be called by their assumed name beyond shift and office hours and even switched to an email address and identity that bore the pseudonym.

> In my office, most of the guys don't know my real name. We call each other by the pseudonym. So most of us forget our original names.

Though some agents were initially upset at having to assume another identity, they accepted it at first as part of job requirements and later as a means of facilitating better performance.

Pseudonyms were instrumental in helping agents cope with racial abuse during calls. That is, they provided agents with a sense of refuge from the backlash of callers who were against offshoring and who abused agents for snatching jobs from the West.

Locational masking, while being similarly perceived by agents as facilitating customer ease and service interactions and as protecting them from customer abuse on racial grounds, precipitated stress. Participants who were required to claim that they were based overseas needed to know enough about their location so that they could answer customer queries. While organizations took care of this via cultural training and regular updates, as discussed earlier, some participants did admit to uneasiness. According to them, since they could not anticipate all the questions customers could pose, it was possible that they may be at a loss at some point in time.

Overall, cultural and linguistic requirements, adoption of pseudonyms and engaging in locational masking, being seen as a part of the job, were accepted within the realm of professionalism. According to agents, it was easier for client and organizational objectives, and, in turn, their own evaluation criteria, to be met, with the assumed identity. Indeed, acceding to these demands did not adversely affect agents' sense of self. Instead, it resembled donning a persona that, in reflecting various characteristics of the customer, allowed service interactions to proceed smoothly, simultaneously putting customers at ease and serving organizational and client objectives. For agents, then, identity posing clearly made their task easier (Poster, 2007), though a few doubted whether such strategies were completely effective, reflecting Taylor and Bain's (2005) view that cultural and linguistic differences are not readily overcome. Some agents claimed that job-related cultural and linguistic requirements, pseudonyms and locational masking augmented their professional identity. They derived pride from their association with overseas clients and customers. Becoming Westernized was equated with sophistication and success in the Indian context (Cohen and El-Sawad, 2007). Nonetheless, the adoption of these national identity management strategies (Poster, 2007) confirms Taylor and Bain's (2005) observation that offshoring is not seamless and clients face a series of problems linked to customer-oriented logic.

Agents encountered a variety of customer reactions in the course of their work. Broadly, customers could be divided into two groups: those who remained unaware of agents' Indian origin and whose responses to agents and their calls ranged from positive to neutral to negative; and those who were aware of agents' Indian origin (either because of the widespread knowledge about offshoring and/or because they had probed such information from the agents) and whose reactions to agents and their telephonic interactions reflected positive, indifferent and negative attitudes. Agents elaborated on the positive and negative responses displayed by the latter group.

Poster's (2007) observation that customers' racial and ethnic animosity took different forms, from subtle comments and sarcasm to explicit comments and cursing, was reported by our participants as well. It was not uncommon for customers to refuse to speak to, transact with or buy anything from Indian agents. Quite often, agents had to face the ignominious situation of customers hanging up. Customers displayed scepticism and cynicism about Indians' ability to help them out, given that India is a developing country. Moreover, they harboured discomfort and distrust about sharing personal and sensitive information, particularly in matters relating to their finances and social security, with people from another country. That they were unaware of how call centres operated within the context of offshoring to ensure effective service delivery came out clearly—they could not understand how agents sitting so far in India could help them out. As Poster (2007) shows, these customers refused to be served by an Indian, and demanded to talk to a 'real' American agent.

> I worked for a US project. The American customers are very rude, they don't like speaking to Indians. The moment they come to know that they are speaking to an Indian, they will bang the phone.

Instances of customers expressing ire over the offshoring trend, holding agents responsible for the unemployment situation in their country, were also frequently reported. Poster (2007) argues that aggressive behaviour by customers may have been prompted by elements of the US media, political rhetoric and popular culture, responsible for creating stereotypes about Indians as well as by an underlying resentment about US jobs going overseas. Similarly, Cohen and El-Sawad (2007) talk of UK customer perceptions that UK employees were losing their jobs to Indians.

> At times, we have people who abuse us. They are not happy about outsourcing and complain that we have taken their jobs. You can't do anything about it.

Indian Christian agents with Western names pointed out customers' disbelief that the former's names were their actual, and not assumed, names.

Customer reactions evoked disappointment, distress and helplessness in agents. Nonetheless, customer abuse was to be handled with professional finesse. At their level, agents could only apologize, while either maintaining focus on the customer's actual problem and attempting to solve it if the customer allowed them to proceed, transferring the call to the client's local office located in the customer's country if the customer insisted, or letting go of the call if the customer wished to hang up.

Agents concluded that racial bias was displayed by about 5 to 10 per cent of their customers. In contrast were customers who were happy to speak to Indians and who indicated a keen interest in and appreciation towards India. Customer communication highlighted positive images of Indians as being technologically savvy and intellectually superior, in addition to culturally and spiritually enriched. In such instances, agents were complimented not only for their services but also for their diction and pronunciation of the English language. Similarly, Poster (2007) has reported that about half the agent–customer interactions were neutral, if not explicitly positive.

Agents' responses to abusive customers (whom agents usually referred to as irate customers) covered various dimensions. Instruction during the training phase prepared agents for such an eventuality.

It was made clear to agents that abusive customers had to be handled with empathy, tact, patience and detachment—even hints of reciprocating customers' negative backlash (whether through abuse in English/an Indian language, non-verbal cues or cutting off the call) would invite termination of employment. Agents were further told that generally customer tirades stemmed from reasons not linked to them (such as long call waiting queues, poor service/product quality which prompted the call, personal stressors, repeated disturbances via phone calls and so on) but were being displaced on to them, and hence they should not take the experience personally. On the contrary, they should allow the customer to calm down and then proceed with the business at hand.

> The way you talk is very important. No profanity. No matter what the customer tells, he may curse you, get very personal with you. You have to keep your cool and it is a part of your job. That guy may be frustrated, he had a bad day, whatever...If you retaliate, you use profanity with them, the company could be sued, and you could be thrown out.

Being able to handle the situation effectively as outlined above was seen as a measure of professionalism and resulted in high performance ratings. Moreover, it was here that the adoption of pseudonyms proved worthwhile—agents were reminded that customers were not shouting at them but at their assumed selves.

Being armed with such training prepared agents for irate customers only at a cognitive level. The initial actual experience of being abused upset all agents, and though they never reacted back to the customer on the call, their sense of distress continued throughout the call and they required some time to recover their composure once the call ended.

> They are very annoyed because their jobs have come here. As a result quite a few have no jobs there. They will be like, 'Oh, you Indians! How do you know how to help me?' It is very personal and it hurts you sometimes. You cannot take the next call because you are so upset. That will shatter you for those few minutes. You cannot do anything about it. You have to go to the next call. It does not happen often. You could have one bad call that could ruin your week and have you upset. But it hurts you so badly—when you are sitting in your own country and you have to listen to this from an outsider. In your own country, you have to be treated so badly.

With experience, agents coped effectively with customer abuse. In fact, Poster (2007) points out that it was quite a sobering experience for her as an American to listen to the steadfast composure and professionalism of Indian employees. Going further, a few agents described how, at times, they and/or their team members would place the phone in mute mode and curse the customer aloud in the presence of team members or press the mute button and enable the loudspeaker so that the team could collectively listen to, make fun of and enjoy the customer's tirade. These collective acts, fused with humour and satire directed towards the customer, served as important means of coping.

Agents accepted organizational directives about customer abuse, recognizing the role of client requirements, organizational survival and process retention in this. Consequently, they concurred with the position that agents abusing customers should be dismissed. Over time, they learnt to distinguish between customers whose rudeness arose due to a genuine problem and customers whose personality predisposed them to anger and irritability. Additionally, in instances where agents' coping broke down, they were advised to take a break and regain their equilibrium so that subsequent task performance was not hampered.

An interesting aspect of agents' experiences was their interactions with Indian customers based overseas. In these instances, once customers knew that the agent they were speaking to was an Indian (either because of the widespread knowledge about offshoring and/or because they had probed such information from the agents), they would behave either in a haughty and arrogant manner or in a warm and sentimental way. According to agents, the former set of responses emerged from customers' sense of superiority at being based overseas in contrast to the agents who, being located in India, were perceived as inferior. The latter set of responses, in agents' views, stemmed from customers' feelings of homesickness and subsequent happiness at being linked to someone Indian. Indeed, in these cases, it was not uncommon for customers to express a desire to continue the conversation in an Indian language and to inquire about current developments in India, and agents had to work hard at convincing customers to use only English and to maintain the call duration, keeping in mind their performance parameters.

> We can't use regional languages with NRI customers. That's not professional.

Absorbing Work-related Strain

The demands associated with call centre work, as elaborated upon in the foregoing sections, precipitate strain in agents. Participant narratives show that this strain essentially arises because of technobureaucratic controls manifest via work conditions, monitoring and surveillance and performance parameters, operationalized in a context that privileges transactional psychological contracts. At the same time, participants' narratives emphasise the significance of professional identity in helping them accept and comply with these control measures. Participants' sense of professionalism not only facilitated the absorption of work-related strain, but in contributing to their experience of well-being, also mitigated the perception of the nature and degree of strain.

Working in night shifts, extending the work day and the work week, maintaining strict shift log in and log out times, shortening and/or cancelling breaks, having to meet quality and quantity standards which involved taking back-to-back calls without a breather and sitting continuously while simultaneously and constantly wearing and managing equipment, and work-life imbalance, adversely affected agents' physical and mental health.

With customers being located in the US, UK, Canada and Australia, employer organizations developed work shifts to match the relevant time zones. This translated not only in agents having to work during the Indian night but also going through periodic changes in their work timings as shifts rotated fortnightly or monthly. Similar to Ramesh's (2004) and Poster's (2007) documentation, temporal adjustments wreaked havoc in agents' biological clocks, resulting in illness. Though most agents' bodies adapted with time, for a few agents, health problems persisted. It is relevant to mention that those whose bodies adjusted to nocturnal schedules found themselves physically compelled to maintain the same schedule on weekly and public holidays.

> I cannot sleep at nights. My body is no longer used to sleeping at nights. Even on holidays, I can't.

For three and a half years, I was continually on night shifts. It was taxing. You will feel tired. You can't sleep during the day. The entire body changes, everything changes.

Aggravating this predicament was agents' inability to leave their seats during the shift. As previously described, the strict observation of shift timings meant that agents could not log out of their systems or leave their seats even to go to the restrooms (if it was an emergency, they had to seek permission from the TL to do so). Uninterrupted call flows, apart from entailing incessant listening and talking which lead to oral and aural complications, necessitated continuous use of various kinds of technology, resulting in sensory-motor problems linked to the visual and auditory systems and repetitive strain injury (RSI). The sedentary nature of the job, coupled with the near absence of any significant locomotion during the shift, caused stiffness, cramps and backaches. Reducing or eliminating breaks interfered with agents' eating habits. Where breaks were permitted, long queues in the cafeteria forced agents to choose fast food or skip their meal/snack in order to log in back in time, affecting their nutrition intake. Extension of the work day and the work week exacerbated health problems. Further, the role of commuting to and from work cannot be ignored. Though employer organizations provided agents with transport, not only were the distances covered long, but the practice of pooling together agents living in spatially proximate localities into one travel pool also extended travel time. The state of India's urban infrastructure added to the problem.

> I think these symptoms were dormant for sometime. But six months back, they got severe. Then I went for a blood check-up and the doctor told me. I don't know how long I was having this. It's just because we don't sleep on time, don't eat on time, we work very hard and the working hours are very long. Minimum is 10 hours work plus 2 hours for travelling, so 12 hours—that too, during odd times of the day. Your shift keeps changing and your biological clock collapses. That's the main reason.

> You cannot take a breather. Basically, you are tied down—until you have your break, you have to take the calls. There will be calls one after another. There is no breather sometimes. You don't even know who is sitting next to you. It is stressful. You cannot ask for a break, because calls are waiting.

You have to finish your job. And everything is logged in that system—our time in, our time out, our schedule.

With agents working during the afternoons–evenings–nights (and having little opportunity to be connected with their extra-organizational social networks during work time) and sleeping during the day, work-life balance was severely disrupted. As observed by a host of researchers (see, for example, McMillin, 2006; Mirchandani, 2004; Noronha and D'Cruz, 2006; Poster, 2007; Ramesh, 2004; Singh and Pandey, 2005), there were problems related to spending time with family members, keeping in touch with relatives and friends and completing household duties. Apart from tasks that could be scheduled during the weekend, managing personal matters such as finances, bills/payments, provisions, personal artefacts, etc., during the week was difficult unless sleep was compromised. Maintaining a social life, even with those living in the same household, and pursuing leisure activities were reserved for the weekend. But here too, organizational demands for team outings, team get-togethers and office gatherings played a hindering role. Declining organizational invitations resulted in disapproval from TLs and other superiors, being perceived as lack of compliance and commitment which affected agents' career prospects. Moreover, the mismatch between Indian public holidays and agents' public holidays (decided by the customer group being served) further cut into agents' opportunities to interact with their social networks. Some participants stated that they had neither seen nor had a meal with their family members for several weeks. Also, they missed family celebrations, gatherings and parties at home during national holidays and festivals. Losing contact with friends was frequently mentioned.

> Now they (participants' children) are 4 years old, so they understand. When I have night shift, they will be sleeping when I leave. And they will ask me why I am going for day shift when the shift changes. Then I make them understand that I am not working in an office which requires a continuous night shift. Sometimes, they want me to be with them and play with them. But I have to make them understand that I have to go to work.

> During night shifts, there are imbalances. One cannot spend much time with the family members. Personal work remains pending because in the day one wants to sleep. One misses family occasions because of work—we do not get Indian holidays but customers' holidays, so it becomes difficult to be in touch with family and friends.

Agents asserted that call centre jobs are suitable for bachelors and spinsters. Spouses of call centre agents often complained that couples did not get time to even speak to each other, given job-related requirements. When both spouses were employed in the same call centre, identical shifts were preferred as such an arrangement allowed the couple to get some time together. Instances where such couples working in different shifts found it difficult to make their marriage work, and hence divorced, were cited.

> I was married. But got separated...She was also in a call centre but we never had any time. We didn't see each other. We never talked. All that led to divorce. Long work hours... lack of communication ruins the relationship.

The experience of physical and mental strain, under the circumstances, was inevitable. Health problems such as loss of appetite, changes in body weight, acidity, nausea, constipation, colds and coughs, diabetes, blood pressure, insomnia, chronic fatigue and drowsiness, anxiety, depression, irritability and cognitive disruptions were commonly reported. To summarize the experience in participants' words:

> We have fever and throat problems and we lose weight. What happens is that you work the whole night and you won't eat properly. You come back in the day and sleep. The whole day, you won't eat anything. You get up in the late evening and have your lunch, breakfast, everything together—one meal a day—and then get ready and go for work. I lost a lot of weight after joining the call centre. Food becomes a big problem. You are given a 30 minutes break in which you have to go, have your meal and come back. It is very difficult. You have a big queue waiting and all that. So sometimes you skip the meal, have some juice and come back.

> As a result of shifts, I developed lot of health problems. I was not able to eat or sleep properly. I lost weight. All the time, schedules change. You are just sleeping or working. There is nothing else in your life. My parents are also little worried. Your immunity goes down. You get frequent colds and backaches. The eating pattern changes. You take lots of junk food, lot of coffee and tea—which is actually bad. Those who do not smoke, drink coffee or tea. They eat lots of chocolate which is not really good. It only gives instant energy, but in the long-term, it really hampers your health.

Reliance on various substances such as tea, coffee, alcohol, nicotine and so on, to facilitate coping with work-related demands, was reported, though it is commonly known that their excessive consumption is maladaptive (Burger, 2004) and not only worsens existing physical and mental health problems but causes other illnesses. In keeping with the findings of McMillin (2006), Ramesh (2004), Singh and Pandey (2005), agents in our study also consumed a lot of tea and coffee to stay awake and remain alert, especially during night shifts. Cigarettes and alcohol served as stress alleviators to reduce the emotional strain associated with performance parameters. Alcohol was also used to counter insomnia.

> I know people who drink after their shifts, because they can't sleep. They booze because they can't sleep or they are unable to cope with stress levels and things like that.

While participants pointed out that they attempted to cope with physical strain and ill-health through medical intervention and maximization of rest and sleep, sick leave to recover from illness was not easily granted. Given the emphasis on mass production, employers laid down strict guidelines about granting leave. While agents with less than six months tenure with the organization were not eligible for any kind of leave, agents whose tenure went beyond six months were expected to plan for and inform about their leave requirements well in advance. Moreover, availing of leave without prior consent was considered to be an unauthorized absence. Employer organizations went to the extent of blocking bank salary accounts of those absenting themselves and refusing to give relieving letters to those who finally decided to quit given the situation. Requests for leave with no notice even during instances of ill-health were examined in the light of expected and/or on-going call volume and targets, and accordingly, were granted or denied. In other words, when the call volume and targets were high, agents were expected to report to duty no matter how ill they were. Agents absenting themselves, whether with or without intimation, were either warned or dismissed. In some organizations, the management kept a strict watch on people taking sick leave, going to the extent of checking out agents' homes or places frequented by them as well as verifying submitted medical certificates.

Even if a person is not well, he does not get sick leave. This is reflected on his balance score card—it affects his report. You can take sick leave but your pay will be deducted. One of my friend's brother working for _____(name of the employer organization) had not taken a single leave for six months, after joining. The first time he took leave for five days, he was asked to compensate by compromising his offs and was not paid for those five days. He was not happy with that so the option given to him was to quit.

Ramesh (2004) echoes these findings, stating that unearthly hours, over-exertion and work-life imbalance take a heavy toll on agents in terms of both mental and physical health and job performance. Deery et al. (2002) second this, pointing out that lack of autonomy, extensive monitoring, prevalence of targets and brevity and infrequency of breaks contribute to call centre work being experienced by many agents as pressurizing and frequently stressful, often leading to emotional exhaustion and withdrawal and to sickness absence and ill-health. Temporal flexibility and extended working hours to meet peaks in customer demand add to work pressures (Taylor and Bain, 2005).

Since all these problems were more common and more severe in US and Canadian processes because of the greater time difference, agents preferred UK and Australian processes.

The UK processes timings are better—evenings from 4 pm to 11 pm or so. So one can sleep at night and have a proper schedule. When I first joined the call centre in the US process, I had night shifts and my health really suffered. My digestive system, everything went off—no breakfast…after work, come home and sleep. Plus no social life. I used to work on Saturdays and Sundays also. We could take off on any 2 weekdays. So no time for family, friends or even for oneself.

Attempting to redress some of these issues with their TLs and other superiors made no difference to the situation. Agents were told that coping with these demands was indicative of being professional.

In short, as Poster (2007) states, employees have much to lose in this scenario including their bodies, their mental stability, their family lives as well as their career trajectories. Taylor and Bain (2005) hold that the deleterious effects of task performance are aggravated by frustration, role confusion, a crisis of expectations and psychological tension experienced by Indian agents as they negotiate the contradictions between their culture, identity and aspirations, and the requirements of service provision for Western customers. In spite of these challenges, agents accept the situation because of their professional identity.

The Privileges of Professionalism

Job-related demands and the strain they engendered were offset by agents' sense of well-being emerging from organizational artefacts, personal remuneration and benefits and organizational processes. Organizational facilities and processes as well as material gains added to agents' notion of professionalism, strengthening their compliance with and commitment to employer organizations and their requirements.

Employer organizations were located in ultra-modern buildings, offering state-of-the-art infrastructure and facilities, as also reported by Ramesh (2004) and Mirchandani (2004). Concrete and glass were aesthetically combined in constructing the outer structure of the buildings while elevators, air-conditioning and artistic interiors characterized by wooden/marble/granite bases, bright lighting, elegant but comfortable furniture, decorative artefacts and electronic gadgets installed for security purposes completed the internal environment. The overall impression conveyed was that of efficiency, progress, class and neatness. Facilities within the office premises included individual lockers, cafeterias with wide-ranging menus at reasonable prices, recreation and de-stress rooms with bean bags, computers with internet access, music systems, televisions, indoor games such as carrom boards, table tennis, chess, pool, etc., video games and reading spaces. Gymnasiums, badminton courts and sleep facilities were also provided by a few organizations. Most employer organizations sought to provide physical work environments of international standards resembling those in the West, with some clients insisting that the call floor be an exact replica of the identical process being executed overseas.

> When the company is in a posh locality or office, with good exteriors and interiors, proper furniture, etc., then the moment a person enters the company, he would feel that he is a professional. That environment makes you feel that. Plus you are in a good post so that also makes you feel that

you are responsible. He feels that he is worth something, the company has valued him. He definitely feels that he is a true asset to the company.

I think the office set-up is very fantastic. The office in America is same like this. The building, the paint, everything is same. The client insisted on this. Plus, the cafeteria is nice—well-designed with good food. Even though you are working in the night, you don't feel it is dark because of the lights and the way the call floor has been set up. In the office, we have fun activities—we have TV, carrom boards, fitness rooms, recreation rooms. We have boating on weekends, we have pool. Those who are stressed out can make use of these things.

Apart from adding to their sense of professionalism, the physical work environment triggered favourable self-comparisons with people in the West and with Indian IT professionals. Moreover, agents considered themselves to be superior to employees in the government/public sector and the traditional industrial and service sectors. According to them, these groups were not only less educated and less motivated than them but also their work involved less skill and low returns. In addition, the physical work environment here was described negatively, highlighting its regressive and decrepit nature.

A government office is a place where papers are piled up and people sit there *aaram se* (leisurely). You need to pass some kind of bill in order to get your work done—people are so relaxed, and there is nothing like a professional environment. In contrast, view the people in a modern, good-looking office that looks so professional, so dignified, so clean, so prominent—automatically even your work sense changes. These buildings actually exude a professional attitude and cause you to feel like a professional—that's what I believe. And these well-designed buildings give you a feeling that you are working in a very dignified organization wherein everything is spic and span, everything is disciplined, and that's why you are a professional. All of us have the feeling to live the way we are in our jobs because this gives us a professional attitude. Even if you look at our pantry cleaners and cafeteria boys, they are so well-dressed, they are so professional.

Gains from the job further nurtured agents' professional identity. Designations attached to call centre agents' tasks such as customer care officer, call centre executive, customer care executive, contact centre representative and customer support executive invoked images of white-collared, professional work and upward mobility, enhancing agents' self-esteem. As observed by Poster (2007), our participants too experienced status enhancement because of association with overseas clients and customers and employment with MNC organizations, where applicable, as well as opportunities to visit client locations in foreign countries for training purposes, where applicable. Moreover, participant narratives underscored the extent to which the ITES–BPO sector, especially global offshoring, had altered India's job market. Employees in this sector, particularly those working for MNC captives, MNC third-party and Indian third-party organizations, received attractive pay packages. In addition to their salary, agents received performance incentives in financial and material forms such as gift vouchers, clothes and accessories, movie and entertainment tickets, landline phone sets, cordless phone sets, mobile handsets, i-pods, DVD (digital versatile disc) players, etc. Various allowances such as food allowance, night shift allowance (for those working in the night shift), transport facilities and medical/health services (including a doctor, a counsellor and a nutritionist on call) formed part of the package.

> The money is good. As a fresher in any company, you won't get this much of money initially. And there are good incentives, pick-up and drop facilities, medical benefits, food. We save a lot of money on travelling. Plus you are paid well and other benefits. So I think it is a pretty good way to start off. And there are growth opportunities in the company—you can always grow because they are looking for people who can perform well.

> If you crack one sale, you will get Rs 50. For the second one, again you will get Rs 50. Within ten days, if I go for 10 sales, I will get Rs 1000. Next 10 days, again Rs 1000. So in a month, I can earn Rs 3000. If you need money desperately, you can work towards getting these incentives—the way you pitch to the customers, the way you handle the customers, you can get sales and earn.

Given the limited employment opportunities for those with a liberal arts/science degree as well as the poor returns at the entry level in many technical/professional fields, it is not surprising that the ITES–BPO sector is widely regarded as the most viable means currently available to achieving a decent quality of life. Agents elaborated on the contemporary lifestyle which, in its inclusion of pubs, discos, parties, weekend outings and credit cards, displayed Western leanings.

Those who had prior work experience in other sectors, which paid meagrely, compared the returns received from both the sectors, highlighting in the process the reasons why the ITES–BPO sector was so much sought after in spite of the challenges it presented. Participants emphasized the sense of independence and self-reliance that their income allowed them, demonstrating changes in their self-concept.

> This boom happening in call centres and BPOs...for a normal graduate, you can't get a job like this. What is this ITES–BPO doing? It's actually getting them jobs very easily. So repeating 10 lines a day, I will get paid Rs 10000–12000—amazing, believe me, it is amazing. Because even a guy who works from morning to evening, say in a garment or textile shop, he wouldn't have been paid even more than Rs 3000 and he can't even live properly. Here you get a good income, plus allowances, transport, good office...So somewhere down the line, independence and self-sufficiency, a good life...

> But again you know, something like this, probably 5 years ago, when graduates used to come out of the colleges, what was there? Nothing. People get Rs 2000–3000. Today, an ITES professional, he will be earning not less than Rs 10,000 a month. It's a big amount and especially for people as young as 22 and 23 years of age.

That agents abhorred nomenclatures such as 'cyber coolies' and 'slaves on Roman ships' (Ramesh, 2004), often used to describe them, testifies to the pride they derived from their professional identity.

The notion of professionalism was seen as being pervasive throughout the organization. Organizational processes were seen as exemplifying the organization's espousal of professionalism. Besides, various initiatives, cited as illustrations of the employer organization's commitment to employees' well-being, were viewed through this perspective. Apart from the type of designations used and the nature of returns provided, the organization's concerns for agents' professional development and career growth were mentioned. Many organizations had tie-ups with educational institutions for business administration and management courses, and agents availing of this opportunity were usually fully or partially funded by their employers. Similarly, agents reported that organizations created avenues for vertical movement. Through internal job postings (IJPs) circulated every quarter, communication about promotion opportunities was shared.

Organizations emphasized that career growth was determined by performance and not by sociodemographic factors, seniority or intra-organizational social networks. Organizational claims that merit and objectivity (a value common among professionals, as noted by Raelin [1989]) influenced promotion decisions were interpreted by agents as testimony of its professional orientation. In addition, the possible pace of movement added to this perception, with agents being told that, for top performers, the transition from an entry level post to a junior level supervisory post occurred within a year of joining the organization. The view that anyone whose performance was superior could quickly move up the organizational hierarchy inspired positive images of the employer in agents' minds, strengthening their loyalty towards the organization and increasing their willingness to accept job-related demands and strain.

Creating an atmosphere of congeniality and camaraderie testified to organization's professional orientation. Fun initiatives at the workplace not only served as evidence of the organization's recognition of work-life balance but also provided opportunities for employees to behave as responsible professionals who knew how and where to draw the line between work and pleasure. By and large, call centre organizations were portrayed by their management as extensions of college where work and enjoyment were combined. While task-related requirements remained unrelenting, concerted efforts were put in to create and maintain a vibrant environment to energize as well as de-stress employees. Various competitions, entertainment programmes, hobby classes, birthday celebrations, festival celebrations, and so on, were conducted during work hours, apart from activities such as team outings, team parties and office gatherings (including picnics, treks, family days, etc.) held during weekly and public holidays. Indeed, organizations employed fun officers, fun squads and event managers to manage these roles. The underlying message here, in addition to those of employer concern for employees, professionalism and work-life balance, was that employers were willing to spend on and invest in employees' well-being. Ramesh (2004) asserts that the portrayal of 'work as fun' and 'workplace as yet another campus' was the central logic through which potential employees were attracted to the ITES–BPO sector.

The informal nature of workplace relationships, particularly between superiors and subordinates, helped to highlight the contours of professionalism. That is, it is common practice to address everyone, including one's superiors, by first name in a call centre organization, thereby downplaying hierarchy and promoting integration. Indeed, agents reported instances where employees were reprimanded for using prefixes such as 'sir' or 'madam' when interacting with their superiors. Yet, behaving disrespectfully and overstepping boundaries is not tolerated.

> We are very friendly with our superiors but that does not mean leniency in performance or disrespect. There are certain limits and one cannot forget that. One has to maintain the professional touch.

The professional approach adopted by call centre organizations extended to employee redressal opportunities. Indeed, call centre organizations prided themselves on the number and nature of grievance avenues they provided their agents with. According to them, in keeping with a professional style of management, openness of communication in terms of content, form, style and route were valued. Therefore, in addition to periodic employee satisfaction surveys, skip-level meetings and open fora with superiors, employees with grievances could approach anyone in the organization whether the CEO (Chief Executive Officer), the TL or someone in between via email, letters, telephone conversations or face-to-face meetings. That the professional atmosphere in the organization precluded the complainant's victimization was strongly emphasized. Under such circumstances, not only did agents feel valued and empowered, considering employers in a positive light and displaying greater commitment to them, but also any third-party intervention including legal protection and collectivist groups were seen as redundant. In other words, with their employers taking such great care of their interests, alternative mechanisms were not required.

> We have an open door policy. If one is not happy with the immediate supervisor, we can go and discuss with the senior management, who will not only give a patient listening, but try to solve the problems.

> We have a very good HR department—if you have any issue or problem, you can just walk in. Even at the agent level, you can talk to the HR manager. And the problem is sorted out right there. If they are not given

an answer, then they will be given an assurance that by this date, we will solve your problem. So that way, there is no chance for them to form a union. There is no requirement. We have all the rights we want.

The influence of the notion of professionalism on agents' attitudes towards collectivization embraces a range of issues and serves several purposes. Perceiving themselves as professionals was the primary reason why agents did not wish to associate with trade unions. That employer organizations were seen as protecting their interests reinforced their position. As participants elaborated, they were professionals armed with superior cognitive abilities, sophisticated skills and a sense of responsibility and commitment to work. As professionals, they could be counted on to perform and deliver optimally and behave rationally and objectively, observing and respecting organizational requirements. In turn, organizations rewarded them. Since organizations valued their professional employees, they took pains to look after their rights and well-being. In such a context, employees had no need for unions. In agents' views, unions were relevant in workplaces where employees' interests were being compromised and basic facilities including redressal mechanisms were not in place or not functional. Employees who were vulnerable because of lack of skill as well as employees who shirked work needed the strength of unions to protect them.

> The idea of unions is very funny because it's an MNC. They know how to handle their employees and situations, they can solve anything.
>
> I have never seen unions in call centres. Probably because in a good company, if you complain it will be solved. So they don't need to make a union and fight together, because the company is affected. Unions are never seen because they give you whatever you want. You have some problem with the cab, you can go and tell the TL and TL will take the issue to higher authority. If the cab driver is drunk, they will take him off. That's the way it works.
>
> I think there is no need because you are getting everything. You have drops and pick-ups, good food, good salary, what else do you want? In factories and all, they have unions because they do not have so many facilities.

Agents also demonstrated an aversion towards the tactics adopted by union activists which, to their minds, were not in keeping with professional behaviour. As some of them specified, call centre agents conducted themselves with dignity, and sloganeering, picketing and striking work were unbecoming of professional demeanour.

> It's not a factory that we can get together and ask for something. We are professionals. We are there to serve the client so how can you form a union? They have unions in government organizations—if something goes wrong, they will go on strike and prevent others from working. I think it's all a mess. I think this type of industry (call centres) does not require that. Every six months, you have your appraisal. If you are good enough, show your performance and earn the position. That's what I feel.

> Unions are simply for people in factories. ITES–BPO professionals are intellectuals. They hold intellectual property which can be exchanged but not snatched away from them. You cannot take it away from me because what I have is what I have. So making a union and fighting for things— I don't agree with that personally.

In any case, agents opined that the presence of unions in the ITES–BPO sector would not augur well for its continuity and growth. Currently, overseas clients appreciated India as an offshoring destination not just because of the superior workforce but also because of the macroeconomic business environment of the country. Collectivist activities would pose a serious hindrance to this conducive environment, resulting in relocation of offshoring to other places in South and South-East Asia and South America. Such a development had micro level consequences for agents as employment prospects would be severely and adversely affected.

Through participant narratives, the negative views that agents held about trade unions came through. While unions' affiliations to political parties were not appreciated, their centralized power structure and undemocratic methods of functioning were also derided.

> Employees should not have a union because it can lead to many problems. We can approach our TL or any superior at any time with any issue, no matter whether it is personal or professional. If there is a union, only the union leader will approach the TL and that all becomes formal. Now we are so informal. So that will be a barrier if we are start a union and it will raise a lot of issues. Even the remotest thing will be raised through the union. And the union leader will get certain power and it will be like other industries.

> I don't think unions will be a good idea here. I have heard so many people suffering because of unions. Because the union leader is saying something and you have to follow that.

Indeed, the agents' position suits their employers. From agents' narratives, it appeared that employers take pains to nurture this stand. Cultivating agents' professional identity is an important step in this direction. Organizations then build on agents' self-concept, highlighting the disconnection between professionalism and collectivization which is strongly associated with blue-collared work in the Indian context. Providing avenues for grievances supports organization's claims, promoting the view that unions are redundant under the circumstances. That employer organizations do not recognize trade unions further complicates the perspective meted out to agents. Agents were even told by their employers that their association with unions could result in their being dismissed from their jobs. Finally, organizations' emphasis that unions would hamper the growth of the Indian ITES–BPO sector, with implications for employment opportunities, seals agents' opinions on the matter.

Hints of Resistance?

That a few agents rely on various outlets to cope with work-related strain was pointed out by some of our participants. Extending the call wrap-up time during which relevant information from the phone conversation is keyed into the system, altering their position in the call distribution queue by pressing the release button on their phone, entering wrong customer email addresses into the system if the call did not proceed satisfactorily (so that feedback could not be obtained from the particular customer), extending restroom breaks, unnecessarily transferring customers' calls and delaying the disconnection of calls were some of the ways in which a few agents got some breathing space.

> Team members are all good friends. We will be talking about a good topic. In the midst of the topic, some call comes. By the time I finish the call, the topic will be over and I miss the conversation. So we play some tricks. If we disconnect the call, what happens is that if the call gets monitored, it

becomes a serious issue. Better than that, do a double click, you are now the last person in the queue...One can at least get some breathing time that way.

After every call, once you finish, then you press the end button and the call is over. The moment the call is cut, the next call from the queue comes in, so you see a *pick call* button on the screen. When you click that on the screen, the call comes through. Some guys, what they do is that at the end of the call, when they get that *pick call* button on the screen for the next call, they won't take it, they just sit. They will just sit quiet and the call is diverted to another person.

We have this Avaya phone where, at the end of every call, you have to write notes, saying this number called for this reason and this is what I did. So this has to be written there. For that, it is a temporary log out off the system. It's not exactly logging out, but it's a pause on the calls coming in. So calls don't come in at that time, we just pause. Press the *pause* again and the calls come in. What these guys will do, even if they don't have anything to write, they just press the *pause* button, so the *pick call* screen doesn't come up at all.

Further, as described in a previous theme, customer abuse was dealt with either by placing the phone in mute mode and cursing the customer aloud in the presence of team members or by pressing the *mute* button and enabling the loudspeaker so that the team could collectively listen to, make fun of and enjoy the customer's tirade.

Sometimes one gets tired of so much work and then, on top of it, a customer starts abusing. So what some people do—they put the customer on mute and curse him back. There he is thinking that we are listening to the scolding but actually we are giving it back to him.

Agents were able to decipher when their calls were being monitored either because of an echoing or beeping sound that accompanied such activity or from the call monitoring data sheet, and they would take special care to ensure their optimal performance during that time. In their own words, 'they played the game once they got a hang of it'.

Monitoring times are fixed for each shift and for each team—one can come to know from the monitoring sheet. So whenever I go into a new shift, I keep a watch for this by studying the monitoring sheet. In the monitoring sheet, it will be there. This call is monitored, by this person, on this day, everything will be there. For different teams, different days, calls get monitored. First week, I will make a note. Second week, I will see again and I will find it to be the same pattern. Last shift, we used to get monitored every Monday. So I knew that. So that day, I will be perfect. Otherwise, I would not bother that much.

Sometimes, agents also helped ease their team members' strain. That is, when agents filled in for TLs who, for some reason, could not monitor calls, they manipulated the entire system by telling their team members to give a list of calls on which they had performed well.

For about three months, I used to complete my shift and used to barge the agents. I have to sit on the TL spot, which the TL has entrusted to me. You won't believe me but I used to barge all the 20 agents on a single process and complete this within two hours. I will come and tell each and every team member before log in, I need four rated calls in which you gave perfect information to the customer. And I would send that in for the performance purposes.

While similar activities have been reported by Bain and Taylor (2000), Knights and McCabe (1998), Taylor and Bain (1999) and Townsend (2005) and have been labelled as resistance (Bain and Taylor, 2000; Knights and McCabe, 1998; Mulholland, 1999 and 2002; Sturdy and Fineman, 2001; Taylor and Bain, 1999 and 2003a), our participants maintain that such behaviour on the part of agents, which is occasional and individualized, does not harbour any anti-work or anti-employer sentiment but serves to release pressure. They go on to state that these behaviours neither detract from nor juxtapose uneasily against agents' professional identity. In other words, agents engage in these activities in spite of their sense of professionalism while also knowing fully well that if their employers discover their behaviour, they would face punishment up to the level of dismissal.

5
Professionalism and the Reinvention of the Trade Union Movement

While collectivization endeavours in India's ITES–BPO sector have been initiated and maintained by Indian and international trade unionists and labour activists representing various industrial sectors, based on their observation of work conditions that impinge on employee well-being, and at times, violate employee rights, these attempts are complicated by agents' professional identity.

As highlighted in Chapter 4, agents' professional identity precluded engagement with collectivization endeavours in the ITES–BPO sector. Believing collectivization to be inconsistent with the basic character of professionalism as well as redundant in instances where employers protect employee interests, agents do not see the relevance of getting organized. Employers' use of the notion of professionalism at the micro and macro organizational levels in order to create and maintain an intra-organizational and extra-organizational environment that questions the need for collectivization, in a bid to ensure the realization of organizational and client objectives strengthens agents' position.

That the ITES–BPO sector falls out of the purview of labour laws, given its professional orientation, is a view staunchly maintained by agents and actively promoted and supported by employers. Interestingly, though this view is false, it is widely held across the country (Banerjee, 2006). Government apathy towards employee work conditions, employee rights and employee interests in this sector allow the situation to go unchallenged. On the contrary, both employer organizations and the state stand to benefit from such an approach since the resultant favourable macroeconomic context attracts more global offshored business.

In such difficult circumstances, trade unions and labour activists seeking to make a difference must grapple with the professional identity of their key constituency. In other words, unionists recognize that winning over agents constitutes the first critical step in their endeavour. Conscientization of agents would naturally and necessarily result in effective negotiations with employer organizations, to which the state cannot remain indifferent.

Acknowledging and working through the complex dynamics involved in the collectivization process, UNITES Professionals (Union for ITES Professionals) has emerged as an independent entity representing the interests of India's ITES–BPO employees. This chapter captures the genesis and development of the UNITES chronologically, highlighting its innumerable challenges, especially those presented by the professional orientation associated with the Indian ITES–BPO sector, and pointing out the strategies by which the union movement must reinvent itself in order to effectively address these challenges and achieve its mandate.

Laying the Foundations

The initial attempts to collectivize in the ITES–BPO sector were linked to similar endeavours in the IT sector, and since the flavour of unionizing in the latter instance influenced the forays in the former case, a background of union organizing in India's IT sector is relevant. Interestingly, attempts to organize Indian IT employees, which continued throughout the 1990s, were initiated by unions based in other sectors. One such effort was made by the International Federation of Commercial, Clerical, Professional and Technical Employees (FIET)—a founding member of Union Network International (UNI), which had tried to organize IT professionals through existing affiliates in India. However, these earlier efforts failed.

Subsequently, in November 2000, the ITPF was formed at Hyderabad and Bangalore with trade unionists from the telecom industry taking the lead. By the end of 2001, ITPF offices were formally opened by members of a UNI delegation to India. The initial financial support was provided by The Swedish Union for Technical and Clerical Employees (SIF). At this opening, speakers outlined the role of ITPF. It was emphasized that though the IT professionals liked the sector they worked in and were high performers, they collectively wanted to advance their careers and hedge against professional risks. Further, it was highlighted that professionals would organize not because they were victims of exploitation or communities of people so adversely affected by their work that they wished to fight their employers but because they sought to address less satisfactory aspects of their work such as restricted opportunity for family time and leisure due to long hours of work. There was a need to protect the interests of Indian IT professionals and UNI was to act as their global guardian (UNI, 2002). A vision of a new type of professional association, different from traditional Indian trade unions, was envisaged. Here, organization primarily meant networking to discuss technology trends, identifying skills and subjects for further training, exchanging experience about the quality of training courses, locating job opportunities and providing tips about career development, and hence the organization representing them had to be radically different (Hirschfeld, 2003). ITPF was encouraged to explore the best ways to meet the needs and demands of its members which would involve creating and developing new types of organizations like WashTech in the USA (Tisza, 2005), the IT Workers Alliance in Australia and Syndikat in Switzerland. The Indian experiment was to serve as an organization model for other emerging high technology clusters such as Malaysia, Singapore, Taiwan, Argentina, Brazil, Israel and central and eastern European countries such as Poland, Romania, Latvia and Estonia (UNI, 2002).

However, not all the IT professionals attending these meetings were immediately convinced of the need for such a forum, arguing that trade unionism was no longer appropriate. The 'trade union' tag was not considered to be apt (UNI, 2002). Not surprisingly, then, ITPF chose not to describe itself as a trade union, a term which it believed could unnecessarily put off some of its potential members, but as a forum furthering professional goals. The uncertainty surrounding ITPF's identity and mandate had implications for organizing IT and ITES–BPO employees.

In the meanwhile, there was a rapid increase in the number of employees in the ITES–BPO sector from 106,000 in 2001–2002 to 348,000 in 2004–2005 (NASSCOM, 2005b), leaving ITPF with little choice but to engage with the employees of this sector. However, the view of employers, employees and the public at large remained unchanged—that unions should not enter the IT and ITES–BPO sectors as their presence would hamper growth. Moreover, since ITES–BPO employees, like IT professionals, drew high salaries, there was no need for negotiations and settlements to be arrived at through the process of collective bargaining as was the case in the old economy industries (*The Telegraph*, 2006). Employees in the emerging sectors, viewing themselves as professionals, were not interested in unions. Responding to the situation, ITPF took the stand that it was against the unionization of IT and ITES–BPO employees as such a development would affect the competitiveness of the industry, and emphatically declared that it was not a union (Hirschfeld, 2005). In February 2007, IPTF's website described it as a knowledge forum dedicated to serving Indian professionals in the IT and ITES–BPO industry, seeking to add value to or further the cause of professionals, contribute towards gender equality, secure suitable legislative enactments including the proper enforcement of legislation and render assistance and guidance through several programmes such as research, lectures, conferences, seminars, workshops, symposia, etc. Its vision was to be the most vibrant, collective and leading platform for persons associated with IT and ITES–BPO sectors while its mission was to serve as the voice of IT and ITES–BPO professionals, enriching, empowering and promoting their interests and contributing to the overall growth of the sectors. Towards this end, it provided counselling services, medical transcription training and workshops to improve personal effectiveness as well as launched skill mapping to assess employees' skill levels and wage indicator programmes (enabling IT and ITES–BPO professionals to compare their salaries with their counterparts in other countries). In short, it aimed at fostering the spirit of togetherness, solidarity, service, networking, cooperation and mutual help so as to inculcate in IT and ITES–BPO professionals a sense of belonging and responsibility towards their fraternity and the general public.

Though ITPF tried to provide its members with educational opportunities (via affiliations with organizations like the Association of

Professional Engineers, Scientists and Managers, Australia [APESMA], labour market services and information (through its newsletters), its functioning bore little resemblance to that of full-fledged professional associations which set educational criteria for membership, adopt codes of ethics for practitioners, protect members from less qualified competitors and engage in political activity to secure licensing and continuing education requirements (Hurd, 2000). However, like most professional associations, ITPF took care to maintain cordial relations with employers, displaying reluctance to get involved in areas of employer–employee interface. As Hurd (2000) states, unions that start out as professional associations tend to place more emphasis on professional matters and downplay union issues. Thus, ITPF came to symbolize an association rather than a union, enacting Hurd's (2000) observation that, as a professional association, it catered to individual needs, trying to draw professionals by providing information, professional development and networking services. In spite of this approach, ITPF's existence represented a duality because of its affiliation to UNI on one hand and its strong links with leaders of India's IT and ITES–BPO industry on the other.

The anti-union position of some of the leaders of ITPF did not have the support of their other colleagues who believed that ITPF had no moral right to be anti-union since it received funding support from Union Network International–Asia Pacific Regional Office (UNI–APRO), a regional branch of UNI, a trade union body. These differences led to a rift between the ITPF leaders, with some of them moving out of the organization to establish the Centre for BPO Professionals (CBPOP), under the aegis of UNI–APRO (UNI–APRO, 2005). A further justification for this separate initiative directed exclusively at ITES–BPO employees was grounded in the understanding that employees' work conditions in this sector were sufficiently distinct from those of IT professionals (Taylor et al., 2008). The CBPOP project was launched in July 2004 with the establishment of two service centres, one in Hyderabad and the other in Bangalore. The basic strategy of the project was to establish contact with ITES–BPO employees, convince them about the need for collective representation by creating awareness of and appreciation for trade unionism, connect them to each other by providing a network base and consolidate this network of professionals into a trade union. These objectives were to be realized at the enterprise, regional and national levels, with an emphasis on developing a free and democratic trade union. Soon CBPOP expanded its activities and opened chapters in New Delhi, Mumbai and Chennai. By March 2005, it claimed to have established contact with more than 2000 employees across the various cities (UNI–APRO, 2005).

While CBPOP worked towards its mandate, its establishment resulted in ITPF hardening its stand towards unions. In the words of the ITPF President:

> One issue that has been affecting us at ITPF is the perceived relationship between ITPF and CBPOP as evinced by the numerous queries we have received from CEOs of BPO companies and call centres, IT professionals and journalists. I would like to clear the misinformation by emphatically stating that there is no connection whatsoever between CBPOP and ITPF/UNI...ITPF is against any unionization of IT professionals within the industry. ITPF is but another organization like Bangalore Management Association (BMA), All India Management Association (AIMA), Lawyers' Association, Chartered Accountants' Association, etc., registered under the Society Act, not under the Trade Union Act. I, as National Chairman of ITPF, would like to insist that no one from ITPF should in anyway be connected with CBPOP and vice–versa. (ITPF, 2007).

Facing Emerging Challenges

While CBPOP faced numerous challenges, the most significant set emerged from ITES–BPO employees' notion of professionalism. At the very outset, most employees contacted by CBPOP ruled out the possibility of forming a union. Not only were they unaware of what the term union meant and how unions functioned, but when these were explained to them, they considered the idea to be strange and alien. As professionals, they neither identified with unions nor saw their relevance. As discussed earlier, in their view, unions were for blue-collared workers being exploited in factories and not for well-qualified people working in professional set-ups which looked after their interests. Indeed, agents in our study displayed great disbelief at suggestions of unions being formed in call centres which they described as progressive workplaces.

That credentialism and professional superiority are dogmatically emphasized in the Indian context (Srinivasan, 1989) came out strongly in agents' positions. Social class origins, coupled with prevailing claims for an elite status to be granted to professionals, were largely responsible for the crystallization of professional and managerial class consciousness based on professional symbolism and solidarity. Call centre employees, having internalized the professional identity, aligned themselves with other professional groups, in particular with IT professionals, ostensibly because of the common link with ICTs. Given this, they saw no relevance for unions which they associated with blue-collared workers. In their view, intelligent, qualified, motivated, responsible and upwardly mobile professionals like themselves, whose jobs involved skill and challenge and provided good returns, whose work environments were modern and chic and whose employers looked after their well-being were not in the same category as factory workers. It was this latter group which lacked abilities, skills, motivation and responsibility, performed unchallenging tasks in dilapidated environments and experienced exploitation that required union protection. Recognizing the deep-seated influence of professionalism on ITES–BPO employees, senior union activists knew what the essence of their strategy for this sector should hinge on. In other words, they realized that ITES–BPO employees were different from traditional union members and needed to be treated as such:

> We need to demarcate these knowledge workers from the traditional union members. These people are special, they feel special about themselves. They are professionals and they are working in very good companies wherein their working style is good, working culture is good...we need to address them professionally...we have to be presentable...why do we call ourselves unions or we should call ourselves associations and project ourselves as professionals so that they accept us.[1]

In fact, as is the case with professional employees (Hurd, 2000), call centre agents in our study maintained that unions were better suited to blue-collar occupations and low wage service work. Accordingly, in their view, unions were relevant to employees working in domestic

---

[1] Participant quotes are included in this chapter to illustrate the various themes. For reasons of confidentiality, participants have not been identified individually.

call centres where work conditions were pathetic. Moreover, with slogan shouting on the streets and picketing ITES–BPO organizations (*Indiatimes*, 2005) being seen as detrimental to their professional image, call centre employees, in keeping with other professional groups, were not convinced that they must assume an adversarial role in advancing their cause (Seidman and Cain, 1964), which would only earn them disdainful titles such as 'blue-collar officers' (Sheth, 1993).

> Before joining the meeting…I thought…I have seen the same CBPOP marching on the roads, holding banners. I think somewhere it was a negative outlook in my eyes, that it is a trade union or something like that.

The link between professionalism and individualism was emphasized as an impediment to unionization. Taking pride in their individual abilities and effort, as is common with professionals (Hurd, 2000), agents drew a link between their contributions to and their outcomes from their jobs. Believing in the relevance of merit as the means of career progress, agents feared that the presence of unions would reverse these trends by introducing a levelling effect through attempts to protect the less capable, compress salary differentials and equalize pay (Kornhauser, 1962). Agents clearly harboured the view that in shielding poor performers, unions discriminated against good performers. With performance being a measure of professionalism, such developments signified a regressive move, deterring agents from endorsing the collectivist endeavour.

Moreover, resistance to unions stemmed from the fact that call centre agents believed that their alignment with a union entails the rejection of key professional values (Raelin, 1989). To elaborate, they associated unionism with a low professional self-image and low standards of professional conduct (Faia, 1976).

In addition, agents were influenced by the anti-union position espoused by their employers. Consequently, they feared adverse reactions, including dismissal, should their employers learn about their links with a union.

> Probably everyone has a fear that if the company knows that we are the part of the union, we will be chucked out.

Responding to agents' fears, senior trade unionists urged ITES–BPO employees to fight for their rights, maintaining that they were protected by law and by a booming job market. Acknowledging that creating a union requires courage, dedication, acceptance of risk and management of employer resistance (Heery et al., 2003), senior trade union leaders reminded the young ITES–BPO employees that, historically, all unions had difficult beginnings which were responsible for the benefits they enjoyed today. Contrasting how private sector organizations mercilessly sacked activists of managerial associations to nip their collectivist endeavours in the bud (Ramaswamy, 1985), senior trade unionists emphasized that today's ITES–BPO employees had the support of a global union federation such as UNI whose 15 million members came from 150 countries and were organized in more than 900 unions. The leaders of various Indian trade unions such as those of Bharat Sanchar Nigam Limited (BSNL), Bank of Baroda and State Bank of India assured ITES–BPO employees of their unstinting support.

Nonetheless, in keeping with Cohen and Hurd (1998), the foregoing exhortations of union leaders and activists allayed ITES–BPO employees' misgivings only partially. Having subscribed to employers' positions that the presence of unions hampers the macroeconomic environment, employees continued to harbour the view that a collectivist agenda is at odds with business interests and pursuing such a path would unleash conflict into a favourable context. Indeed, management's subtle references to conflict come out at this juncture, through their contention that the presence of unions creates tension, anxiety and disruption because of the use of strike and job action (Cohen and Hurd, 1998). In the case of ITES–BPO employees, employers propagated that the formation of unions would only threaten the flow of foreign direct investments into India (*Outsourcing Times*, 2005), spelling disaster for the fledgling ITES–BPO industry in the country. They went on to highlight that India has achieved a significant milestone in this industry because of the absence of unions (Nahar, 2006), and hence third-party intervention did not augur well for its future (Iype, 2005). By juxtaposing the unsavoury picture of union-related conflict and its consequences with the attractive image of peace and cooperation in the absence of unions based on promises of improved employer–employee communication and an increased voice for employees (Cohen and Hurd, 1998) and concomitant prosperity, employers tried to avert union formation. It is not surprising, then, that call centre agents in our study came to believe that union formation would only precipitate problems for employer organizations, clients and employees themselves, threatening the continuity of the industry and, in turn, of their own employment. Undoubtedly, the very nature of capital enabled employer organizations to propagate this view among agents. Having been abused by overseas customers over the offshoring trend and its implications for the job market in their countries and observing the growing threat posed by emerging offshoring destinations in Asia and South America (Noronha and D'Cruz, 2006), agents seconded the truth of their employers' claims. Staying away from unions and avoiding conflict, even in instances where their rights were violated, was the preferred option, and hence it was not uncommon to find ITES–BPO employees quitting their current jobs and seeking fresh appointments within India's booming ITES–BPO sector rather than engaging third party intervention to redress their grievances.

Overall, the ITES–BPO employees' stand was similar to NASSCOM's position that unions are irrelevant to ITES–BPO sector employees as employers observe standard norms (NASSCOM, not dated a) in providing exceptionally good work environments, salaries (Jha and Chatterjee, 2006) and benefits, besides allowing employees direct access to their CEOs (Jayanth, 2007) in case of grievances, a view which was also endorsed by Mr Ameet Nivsarkar, Vice President, NASSCOM, when we interviewed him on 26 February 2008 (Noronha and D'Cruz, 2008a). Advocates of this philosophy negated the role of unions while emphasizing that sophisticated human resource management (HRM) strategies have a significant potential to take care of the interests (Nahar, 2006) of educated 'executives' who have a voice of their own (*Financial Express*, 2005).

Undoubtedly, ITES–BPO employees' professional identity precipitated in them apathy towards unions. In contrast, literature describes professionals' ambivalence towards unions (Hurd, 2000). In the Indian context, this dilemma was reflected in the behaviour of bank officers who claimed the status of professionals but craved for the protective status of workman under the Industrial Disputes Act, 1947 (Ramaswamy, 1997: 179).

ITES–BPO employees' apathy towards unions got reflected in their attendance at meetings, with CBPOP activists finding it extremely difficult to mobilize them. Through repeated interaction with these employees over an extended period of time, CBPOP office bearers were able to convince a few of them of the relevance of unions. Yet, even in these instances, employees expressed reluctance to be publicly associated with unions and those agents who attended union meetings strove to maintain the secrecy of their association with CBPOP.

However, by the end of July 2005, CBPOP took the initiative to register a trade union at the national level but failed in its efforts due to government indifference towards unions in general. Nonetheless, by this time, the groundwork for the founding convention of the first union in the ITES–BPO space in India to be held on 18 and 19 September 2005 was completed.

At the helm of affairs were senior trade unionists and labour activists who had started CBPOP and were linked to unions in other sectors in India and to UNI–APRO as well as a few ITES–BPO employees who were convinced of the need for collectivization while maintaining their professional identity and harbouring the fear of employer reprisal should their links with the prospective union become public. Importantly, the new union had to quickly realize that unionization and professionalism were not inherently incompatible (Raelin, 1989), particularly since the unionization of ITES–BPO employees would definitely be determined by their professional identity (D'Cruz and Noronha, 2006).

Resolving Identity Issues

During the founding convention (as well as at prior meetings), issues relating to the name of the organization were fiercely debated. ITES–BPO employees of all the CBPOP chapters unanimously agreed that the word 'association', rather than the word 'union', should be used to describe their collective. In their view, the word 'association' had multiple advantages. Firstly, the negative connotations linked to the word 'union' would be put aside. Over time, Indian trade unions had acquired unfavourable reputations of behaving irresponsibly, catering to vested interests, adopting disruptive tactics, neglecting the concerns of members and ignoring the welfare of society at large (Sheth, 1993), and the prospective union was keen to distance itself from such an image.

Moreover, employers were more likely to accept an association as compared to a union. As Hurd (2000) asserts, employers do not object to employee involvement with professional associations but they may be extreme in their opposition to unionization. Reminisces of this could also be observed in India wherein professionals did not want to be called trade unionists in order to gain the acceptance of the management (Ramaswamy, 1997). To this end, the prospective union understood that to declare itself as a full-blown trade union, particularly during its infancy, might leave it isolated from potential supporters and vulnerable to employer repression (Taylor and Bain, 2008).

Finally, given that the ITES–BPO industry was seen as ushering in a new age into India, the use of the term 'association' cohered with this fresh start.

Not surprisingly, then, ITES–BPO employees who were involved in the genesis of the new union suggested names such as All India ITES Professional Association, All India Association for BPO Professionals, Indian ITES Professional Association or the New Age Economy Professionals.

> The word union has a negative image in itself. So it's important not to call it a union but an association.

ITES–BPO employees and senior union leaders also struggled over whether an ITES–BPO union should include employees engaged in allied/support services such as transport, cafeteria, etc., situated within this sector. ITES–BPO employees believed that these groups were not professionals like themselves and hence should not be included. However, experienced unionists, owing to the strong criticism of the neglect of the informal sector by trade unions (See Noronha, 1996; Sheth, 1996) did not concur with this view. Though a debate ensued about the propriety of both arguments, the allied/support staff were finally left out.

ITES–BPO employees back their position by insisting that their professional status distinguished them from the allied/support staff and warranted exclusive representation.

Membership is for the professional. There is no other staff. The drivers are outsourced, security is outsourced, housekeepers are outsourced, food contractors are outsourced. Allied staff are not going to be a part of this union.

Their stand is reflected by Seidman and Cain (1964) and Strauss (1964) who note that professionals split off from an existing all-inclusive organization to form one limited to professional employees, ridding themselves of blue-collar leadership. ITES–BPO employees exhibited a high degree of status consciousness, desiring to keep fellow employees who lacked their credentials out of their organization. This behaviour is not new to the Indian context, being documented by Srinivasan (1989) who states that the Indian case is a paradoxical mix of professional chauvinism and instrumental liberalism, on account of which the professional union movement had, by and large, not joined hands with the trade union movement, except on vital issues.

While working within the purview of ITES–BPO employees' professional orientation, senior union leaders simultaneously challenged it. They often urged employees to get rid of the illusion and manipulation of being a professional and focus on the issues at stake, namely, that of decent work and dignity at work. They underscored that terms like 'professional' or 'executive' (*Financial Express*, 2005) were only used to circumvent the law and strip employees of job security and sometimes of even occupational status. They further pointed out that organizations have been redesigning occupations and designations to suit the flexibilization programme, thereby taking away many stipulated rights designed for specific categories of workers. In keeping with this agenda, the earlier 'office clerk' is now designated as 'junior management executive', 'supervisor' as 'production executive', 'worker' as 'knowledge technologist' and so on (Banerjee, 2006). Such insidious designs, senior unionists held, made it imperative for ITES–BPO employees to join trade unions and protect their rights and interests. Instead of being ashamed of such associations, employees should be proud to join a union which allows them to be at par with their employers. In their view, it was important for employees to recognize that it was poor leadership that was responsible for the sorry state of unions in India and that the institution itself retained its relevance.

> I don't like people telling me, ah, we are professionals. One should see how the word is used. Even if you are a professional and not treated as a professional, you are still an employee, you may have the illusion that you have the title. Now every company is manipulating this provision in the law to create artificial names and positions so that the person is automatically excluded from labour laws…The strength is not in the real name that we get, but it is in the real dignity that we get. There is no need to apologize or be ashamed…we have to ask ourselves what is wrong with the present union…we cannot say that we don't want a union. It is not the question of choice, it is a question of necessity and need.

Senior unionists highlighted that if Indian Airlines's and Air India's pilots were workmen under the Industrial Disputes Act, 1947, then ITES–BPO employees could also be covered by the same definition and receive similar protection. They opined that a monthly salary of Rs 10,000 to Rs 15,000 did not debar ITES–BPO employees from being covered under the Industrial Disputes Act. Citing the case of the banking sector, senior unionists pointed out that bank officers were also unionized and did not come across as mesmerized by the designation and formal insignia of 'managers' (Ramaswamy 1997: 179). In fact, militant unionization among engineers, doctors, bank officials, lawyers and teachers in India had become a regular form of middle-class politicization (Srinivasan, 1989).

Pursuing this line of argument, senior leaders indicated that regardless of the name of the union, its mission would remain the same. Referring to APESMA, senior unionists stated that though this association was registered under the Trade Union Act, it involved itself in collective bargaining as well as service provision.

> It is nothing to be ashamed of if you say you are a part of a union…. Some of them call themselves as association, some trade union. For instance, APESMA, an association of professionals in Australia, is registered under the Trade Union Act. We have a union which represents nuclear scientists, we have engineers, doctors.

Notwithstanding the animated and prolonged debates described above, the name finally chosen for the nascent organization reflected the professional orientation of its primary stakeholders. As one senior unionist stated:

We told them (the ITES–BPO professionals) that we will appreciate your ideas—that is why we do not force anybody to call yourself unions. You may strive for the same thing like unions do, but call yourself anything else. That is why we decided that a centre for call centre employees and professionals be established, instead of calling it a union.

While the initial name was UNITES (Union for ITES Employees, which included acronyms such as UNI and ITES), the ITES–BPO employees present at the founding convention continued to feel uncomfortable with the word 'union'. The President-designate voiced this concern at the time of making her acceptance speech at the founding convention:

I have slight problem definitely with the name—because it was just shown, and in a quick move, we had to accept it. Individually, as a BPO professional, I cannot relate to the name. How do I expect so many thousands of BPO employees to go along with this name? The very word union hooks off any youngster…it has to be something that they can relate to, we have to think about it. CBPOP is a better option.

To overcome this stalemate, the appendage 'professional' was added to UNITES embracing both the 'union and professional association in its name—UNITES Professional' (UNI, 2008). UNITES Professional (henceforth referred to as UNITES) was headquartered in Bangalore, with chapters in Mumbai, New Delhi and NCR, Chennai, Hyderabad and Cochin.

Partnering Employers

Senior union leaders associated with UNITES recognized the importance of having to work within the framework of ITES–BPO employees' espousal of the professional identity. Indeed, they were faced with the challenge of how to perform the functions of a professional association while simultaneously embracing unionism. They realized that union organizing needs to be built around a positive image of enhanced voice rather than a negative image of waging conflict to whip the boss into shape (Hurd, 2000). Thus, the combination of desire for voice, aversion to conflict, preference for cooperation and concern about preserving individualism presented a challenging mosaic for leaders who hoped to build consensus for collective action (Cohen and Hurd, 1998) among ITES–BPO employees.

Responding to these circumstances, senior unionists acknowledged the need to move away from the conventional protest and grievance handling functions of unions to engage in partnership with management. They foresaw unions as having a much larger role to play in solving a wide variety of workplace problems, including attrition. Therefore, the union that was being conceived was to be a constructive entity, beneficial to all the stakeholders, including employers. UNITES was to operate from the standpoint of cooperation and responsibility, rather than militancy and aggression, so that 'mutual gains' were secured for all the stakeholders. The interest of the industry and the workers went hand in hand and employees had to be flexible and accommodating of employers' needs for the industry to survive. Accordingly, productivity was emphasized and extreme Leftist leanings were denounced. This strategy was expected to rebuild the credibility of Indian unions as respectable, credible, dignified and responsible groups which ITES–BPO employees would be proud to be a part of.

> It is not that a union should be formed when there are disputes. My understanding of the union is very different. Union can play a constructive role, even complementary role, with the industry, with the management—it could work with the company to develop so that we can contribute, prosper and share...We should take away the misconception. We should bring back an understanding so that the union leaders do not see themselves as grievance handlers but as partners.

Emphasis on social dialogue rather than protest as means to resolve disputes formed a significant part of UNITES's agenda. The main goal of social dialogue was to promote consensus building and democratic involvement among the main stakeholders in the world of work. Successful social dialogue structures and processes had the potential to resolve important economic and social issues, encourage good governance, advance social and industrial peace and stability and boost economic progress. UNITES further believed that dialoguing with NASSCOM was required to make India's ITES–BPO industry more sustainable.

In a nutshell, UNITES resolved to be a partner in management, involved in the good governance of the industry. This conscious avoidance of unnecessary adversarialism and hostility to employers, which were redolent of an inappropriate conflictual style of trade unionism, was seen to progress the interests of the industry and to attract members (Taylor et al., 2008).

> My submission at this point of time is how are we going to create credibility for such associations—a union or any name you pronounce for such activity—how are you going to create a credibility? The overall atmosphere is not in favour of the unionization.

While all UNITES members subscribed to the aforementioned plan of action, a few of them expressed doubts as to whether employers would be interested in such a partnership. Two reasons were put forth to support these misgivings: first, employers' claims that their HR policies and working conditions, including remuneration, rendered unions redundant; and second, employers' opinion that the best way forward for the ITES–BPO industry was to dissociate themselves from unions, thereby gaining a free hand at the workplace.

Reconciling Servicing and Organizing

UNITES's office bearers remained clear that engaging constructively with industry did not amount to being co-opted by them. On the contrary, UNITES would retain its distinctive role in representing employees. The key to success was to reinforce the image of the union as a professional organization that can deal with management on its own level, but on employees' terms (Hurd, 2000). UNITES made it clear that it would not hesitate from championing issues of employee rights, justice, fairness and corporate social responsibility and it would continue to represent employees with genuine grievances against their employers (Taylor et al., 2008).

Further, globalization required employees to have a strong voice and UNITES remained committed to this end. Since offshoring had pitted employees of different nationalities against each other, UNITES believed that the only way forward was for employees to come together and convince employers to rethink their strategies in favour of development that was sustainable for all. Present policies that suggested a race to the bottom were not in the best interests of employees, customers, national economies or sustainable development. Instead of responding to employer initiatives to relocate work overseas with arguments that could be misconstrued as racist, xenophobic or protectionist, the thrust required was that of decent work for all. According to UNITES, the only way to ensure compliance with decent labour standards was for employer organisations and UNI to establish global framework agreements which included clauses on employees' rights, union rights, health and safety, elimination of discrimination, minimum wages and working conditions, employment stability, respect for others at work and respect for the environment.

At the ground level, UNITES applied the fundamental principle of the organizing model (Taylor and Bain, 2008). UNITES's chapters set themselves membership targets and agreed to a regular exchange of ideas and views including organizing periodic state and national conventions, promoting centres and web-based interaction, conducting training in organization development and developing a core set of leaders who would be trained in various laws and skills of collective bargaining. Among UNITES's notable interventions are its campaign for employee safety in the aftermath of the tragic rape and murder of Bangalore-based Hewlett Packard employee Pratibha Murthy and the representation of employees of the Bangalore-based company BelAir who had been summarily dismissed without pay. UNITES also succeeded in negotiating four collective bargaining agreements (Excel Outsourcing Services, e-Merge Business Processing, Infopoint and Transact Solutions), although these breakthrough arrangements are confined to small and medium enterprises (SMEs) in the domestic sector and the aim of securing collective bargaining in international facing operations has yet to be realized. Clearly, UNITES has established a genuine, if limited, presence in Indian ITES–BPO, raising questions about NASSCOM and the industry's assertion that the independent representation of employees is unnecessary and unwanted in the Indian ITES–BPO environment (Taylor et al., 2007).

At the same time, UNITES has taken cognizance of its links to professionalism and, accordingly, its activities have embraced the servicing model of collectivist endeavours. Hurd (2000) states that an information-intensive approach to organizing, which addresses professional issues as well as workplace developments, has the potential to attract support from employees. Clearly, there is potential in unions embracing certain practices of professional associations as part of an effort to lay the foundation for eventual unionization. Along with organizing, then, UNITES aimed at becoming a forum that could reflect the professional aspirations of its key constituency. UNITES took on board some of ITPF's ethos and orientation. Its members wished to develop UNITES as 'a community of professionals', which would ensure that it provided educational and training services as well as information and advice (Taylor and Bain, 2008). The services envisaged were good psychiatric support, counselling services and yoga/fitness clubs to promote members' well-being, career development, financial services, group health insurance, placement consultation and legal support. UNITES was expected to establish a core certification programme with leading educational institutions like NIIT and Aptech, at the national level, for both employees and students, not only to draw people towards the association but also to establish the association's credibility. Interfacing with professional bodies such as HR fora, the Computer Society of India and the Manufacturing Association of India were foreseen as building the brand image of UNITES. A newspaper called 'Call Centre Voice' was to be published to reach out to all ITES–BPO employees.

The unity of the organizing and the servicing models of union activity has become all the more promising with ITPF and UNI–APRO renewing their ties in February 2008. It raises hope of better coordination and cooperation in meeting the objectives of the ITES–BPO employees. While ITPF could concentrate on providing services to ITES–BPO employees, UNITES could continue to organize. In this manner, the potential for professional associations to move towards unionization as well as for unions to evolve towards professional associations can be exploited (Raelin, 1989).

> Many people because of their bad experience and bad impression about unions never want to join a union. So they need an alternative whereby their interest can still be represented. I think, in the long run, ITPF and UNITES can complement each other.

The formation of UNITES proves, without doubt, that the union organizing and servicing models are not mutually exclusive (Fletcher and Hurd, 1998) but supplement each other, providing the greatest opportunities for convergence (Hurd, 2000). Thus, as Taylor and Bain (2008) argue, in all likelihood, UNITES's future success depends on its ability to straddle the contradictions involved in providing a network for ITES–BPO employees—that is, acting like a conventional trade union in the making while simultaneously developing forms of community unionism.

6

Professionalism Contested

That employer organizations engage the appeal of professionalism as a means of identity regulation and socio-ideological control is reinforced by the academic debate linked to the sociology of the professions and by managerial views on the role of professionalism in the Indian call centre industry. This chapter, in the two sections which follow, captures these dimensions.

The Academic Debate

The following section situates the notion of professionalism as delineated by our participants against the concept of professionalism as elucidated within the taxonomic and power approaches of the sociology of the professions. Notwithstanding Evetts's (2006) view that the contemporary framework of the appeal of professionalism has rendered the traditional taxonomic perspective redundant, we examine call centre agents' narratives in the light of the taxonomic and power approaches. Following an elaboration of the two perspectives, we juxtapose the conceptual view vis-à-vis participants' definitions of professionalism, highlighting similarities and differences. Through this analysis, employer organizations' engagement with the appeal of professionalism as a means of identity regulation and socio-ideological control as well as the gap between rhetoric and reality (see Chapter 7 of this book for a discussion) come out clearly.

Conceptual Issues

Occupations that perform tasks of great social value because those enacting them possess knowledge and skill that in some way set them apart from other kinds of workers and that entail a self-regulating form of social control are known as professions (Freidson, 1984). While those who perform the tasks associated with the professions are called professionals, they also display the characteristics expected of the members of specific professions (Middlehurst and Kennie, 1999). According to Freidson (2001), professionalism not only embraces the belief that certain work is so specialized as to be inaccessible to those lacking the required training and experience and the belief that such work cannot be standardized, rationalized and commodified, but also represents the occupational control of work where workers enjoy the autonomy to organize and control their own work as against customer or managerial control where customers or employers choose who is to perform what tasks and how much will be paid, on what terms, for performing them. Professionalization captures the process whereby work groups attempt to actually change their position on one or more dimensions of the occupation–profession continuum, moving towards the professional pole (Pavalko, 1971). Numerous discussions on 'emergent professions', 'professions in transition' and 'professions in process' represent different ways of referring to and identifying the process of professionalization.

Dietrich and Roberts (1999) cite literature to highlight two traditional sociological approaches to the understanding of the professions, namely, taxonomic approaches and power approaches.

The taxonomic approach asserts that professions are a special category of occupations which possess unique attributes that distinguish them from non-professional occupations. Within this approach, trait approaches list attributes that are not theoretically related but which are seen to characterize professions while structural–functional approaches focus on attributes that are seen to be functional to the wider society (Dietrich and Roberts, 1999).

The trait model of professions includes two core characteristics—a body of theoretical and technical knowledge and a service orientation. On the basis of these characteristics, the profession claims and acquires other properties. This includes professional autonomy which is the right accorded by society to members of a profession to determine the nature of problems with which they will be concerned, the appropriate procedures by which these should be solved and the evaluation of professional performance. In addition, the professions are characterized by control over recruitment and licensing of new members, a long period of training and socialization, monopoly over the performance of certain tasks, authority recognized by clients and the public, a belief in the importance of their function, a sense of community, formal associations and a code of ethics (Latham, 2002; Leicht and Fennell, 2001; Toren, 1975).

According to the structural–functional view put forward by Parsons, the professions are associated with an expert authority which is instrumental in maintaining modern society. Using their knowledge and skills which are unavailable to non-professionals, professionals operate as double agents or interstitial go-betweens, mediating between individuals—their customers—and society as a whole. On the one hand, they use their authority to curb their own customers' deviance and to align their customers' interests and actions with broad social norms. On the other hand, they use their authority to create safety zones for individuals against the demands of social norms. Professionals, in the Parsonian lens, constantly invoke their authority to negotiate and re-negotiate the normative boundaries between individuals and society (Latham, 2002).

In Parsons's view, this project of interstitial negotiation is successful only when professionals maintain a certain outlook. They must not be too strongly motivated by the desire for power, lest they attempt to achieve it by promoting social norms at the expense of individual liberty. Similarly, they must not be too strongly motivated by profit, lest they allow their authority to be bought by wealthy private customers seeking exemption from social norms. Instead, professionals' desire for status and reputation both among their peers and in society are key to the success of the professional project. Parsons further pointed out that when professionals are appropriately motivated, then societies, clubs, university departments and publications emerge as their powerful socializers. Though these institutions emerge after the professionals appear, they ensure that professional authority is exercised for social good (Latham, 2002).

To summarize, the structural–functional view maintains that the professions are a special category of occupations which are assigned a reasonable, even generous, level of status and material rewards in return for an undertaking of non-exploitation (the presence of an ethical code), the maintenance of standards of training and qualification and other guarantees to society (Crompton, 1990).

Several authors questioned the utility of the taxonomic attempts at constructing lists designed to differentiate professions from non-professions (see Evetts, 2006). According to Dietrich and Roberts (1999), taxonomic approaches provide mere descriptions of professions rather than bases for analysis. The approach is not considered to be sufficiently dynamic or process-oriented. That is, it takes no account of the unequal distribution of power between the professionals and the customers of professional services but sees the relation between the professions and society as an exchange. The professions provide specialized knowledge and skills and, in return, are rewarded with autonomy, high income and status. The taxonomic approach obscures the historical conditions under which occupational groups become professions (Dietrich and Roberts, 1999). Moreover, the Parsonian view ignores the exploitative actions of professional monopolists who desire status, money and power as well as the failure of professional institutions to guarantee the quality of their members' work (Latham, 2002).

The revisionists rejected the idea that professions can be distinguished from other expert occupations on any empirically essential or analytically invariant grounds. They instead increasingly proposed that professions are simply expert occupations that happen, by one strategic means or another, to establish and maintain particularly well-patrolled, yet structurally unnecessary, monopolies in the labour market for expert services (Sciulli, 2005). Thus, instead of concentrating on abstract traits of an occupation, it was necessary to recognize that resources contributing to successful professionalization stem from linkages to the wider social structure (Klegon, 1978). The analytical focus shifted from professions as central functional structures in society to the study of professionalism, professionalization and professional projects (Henriksson, 2006). These post-functionalist studies of the professions have tended to see the professions as centres of power claiming exclusive ownership of particular areas of expertise and to raise the status and prestige of their practice while subjecting the public and other occupations to their dominating rules (see, for example, Abbott, 1988; Freidson, 1970; Johnson, 1972; Larson, 1977; Macdonald, 1995).

Examining available literature, Dietrich and Roberts (1999) point out that the power approach to understanding the professions states that the distinguishing feature of the professions is purely their ability to gain societal recognition as professions. The Chicago School of symbolic interactionism believes that the professions are the same as other occupations and profession is merely a title claimed by certain occupations at certain points in time. Occupations seek professional status in order to gain the associated recognition and rewards. The relevant question is therefore not to determine what a profession is in an absolute sense but to consider how society determines who and what is professional.

The main work within the power approach is either the Marxist analysis or the neo-Weberian perspective. While the Marxist analysis of the professions centres on the social relations of production and has emerged from the need to locate the middle classes in the class system, there is a broad spectrum of opinion concerning the position of professionals. On the one hand, professions are seen as fulfilling the global functions of capitalism. On the other hand, they are seen as subject to proletarianization and deskilling, gradually losing status and power. Professions are at a contradictory location within class relations, sharing characteristics with the exploited and exploiters. Professional groups attempt to use their power as exploiters to gain entry to the dominant exploiting class, and this, in turn, strengthens their professional position (Dietrich and Roberts, 1999).

The neo-Weberian literature focuses on market conditions, viewing society as an arena where competing groups struggle with each other and with the state to gain status and power. Conflict is a catalyst for change and the segmented nature of occupations that strive for professional status is crucial to this process. Segmentation creates a diversity of needs and wants which are central to forming an occupation's experience of professionalization. The struggle for control is facilitated through social closure which is employed by professional groups to defend their privileged position. Professionals struggle to achieve market control by restricting entry to a limited group of eligibles, eligibility being based essentially on credentialism and often backed by legislation (Dietrich and Roberts, 1999).

The power approaches are explicitly dynamic and necessitate historical analysis whose central focus is the recognition of the power sources utilized by occupations in their struggle to achieve and maintain professional status and the way this power is institutionalized within the emerging profession (Dietrich and Roberts, 1999).

In spite of the caveats associated with the taxonomic approach, it remains highly influential (Glasner, 1979). Indeed, as Klegon (1978) states, the characteristics that are used to define professions operate as strategies for the achievement and maintenance of a particular level of occupational status that grants power and prestige to its practitioners. That is, the special knowledge and skill used to define the professions are a part of a political process claimed by the group to advance its interests. For Freidson (1970), the autonomy and control characteristic of the profession rests on esoteric knowledge and on patronage. Without both the peculiar knowledge and the protection and sponsorship of that most powerful patron, the state, the autonomy which characterises professionalism cannot be achieved. Similarly, in Larson's (1977) view, such knowledge was necessary for the original professionalization project, which endeavours to translate one order of scarce resources—special knowledge and skills—into another—social and economic rewards. In the absence of such knowledge, the profession's monopoly becomes the monopoly of nothing. Professionals, being processors of knowledge, form themselves into a group, which then begins to standardize and control the dissemination of the knowledge base and dominate the market. This enables them to be in a position to enter into a 'regulative bargain' with the state. Professions have been careful to protect their expertise via the activities of associations who control the recruitment and training of new entrants, defining levels of competence, and protecting their special knowledge base through mystification and the conduct and standards of work by individual professionals (Devine et al., 2000; Klegon, 1978). Thus, the association of professionals is central to the interests of monopoly. The significance of these institutions lies in their exclusionary power, that is, their ability to close a profession's jurisdiction to outsiders (Abbott, 1991).

Wilensky (1964) analyzed the order of various events of professionalization: a substantial number of people begin doing on a full-time basis some activity that needs to be undertaken, the foundation of a training school, the forming of a professional association, the association engages in political agitation to win the support of law for the protection of the group and the establishment of a code of ethics. Similarly, Caplow (1964) identified a sequence involving the establishment of a professional association, the change in the name used to identify the group, the development of a code of ethics and the agitation for and attainment of the enactment of legal restriction on who may or may not perform the services and activities that the group claims as their exclusive domain. However, Abbott (1991) states that the professionalization process is not a simple collective action by a cohesive group but must be recognized as a multilevel, contagious and complex social process. The first event is the rise of an association among professionals. Another event of importance is the profession's attempt to dominate its area of work. A third event in professionalization is the rise of a concern for education. A fourth event of importance is the rising concern for professional knowledge. Some others stress that power is the critical variable in the professional phenomenon. Seeking political legitimation and the development of codes of ethics are typical image-building efforts. A particular customer-serving occupation for establishing a claim to professional status has to have two sources of power: the nature of the service itself and image-building activity. The process involves the formation of set of beliefs by the public that an occupation performs an essential, exclusive and complex service. Successful public recognition is likely to result in a grant of autonomy. Those occupations in which members exhibit autonomy from both customer and employer organization are designated true professions (Forsyth and Danisiewicz, 1985).

The rapid spread of the forms of professional organization among occupational groups which are not professions was observed many decades ago by Marshall (1962). Later, Friedson (1970) remarked that the nomenclature 'profession' was slowly being claimed by virtually every occupation that was seeking to improve its public image. As a high degree of technical competence, sophistication and complexity became increasingly characteristic of the vast majority of work activities, even the most unlikely occupations posed themselves as candidates for professionalization (Pavalko, 1971). In fact, Wilensky (1964) predicted that professionalism would eventually embrace everyone with some claim to specialized knowledge or practice. Others argued that it was not technical competencies alone that were claimed but occupations also claimed professional status by announcing that they were trustworthy, had a code of ethics and a professional association and performed important services which only they were qualified to do, and were therefore deserving of autonomy and prestige (Crompton, 1990; Klegon, 1978). The spread of this phenomenon led Larson (1977) to ask why and how a set of work practices and relations that characterized medicine and law came to become a rallying call for a whole set of knowledge-based occupations in very different employment conditions. Evetts (2006) holds that the contemporary appeal of the discourse of professionalism in all occupations is now widespread and serves as an important control mechanism at work (Fournier, 1999).

Viewing Indian Call Centre Agents through the Taxonomic and Power Approaches

To begin with, there does appear to be some general consensus that a profession is based upon a body of knowledge of an intellectual nature (Snider, 1963). The expertise possessed by professionals is said to consist of a set of esoteric and abstract principles that have been mastered and organized by the profession into a theory under its exclusive control (Baer, 1986; Khurana et al., 2005). Theory serves as a base in terms of which professionals rationalize their operations in concrete situations. Preparation for a profession, therefore, involved a considerable preoccupation with systematic theory, a feature virtually absent in the training of non-professionals (Greenwood, 1962). Further, a system of licensure is available to the professions in order to establish certain standards of proficiency and ensure that at least a minimum degree of competence exists. Usually, examinations conducted by professional associations or by the state must be successfully completed before being allowed to practice a profession (Snider, 1963). Interestingly, while our participants considered themselves professionals, none of these features were present in their case.

To elaborate, though call centre agents considered themselves in possession of superior cognitive abilities and advanced qualifications, performing highly skilled jobs, in reality, in mass customized call centres such as those included in this study, job design elements were characterized by low autonomy, low complexity and low variety, and hence the skills required for task performance included computer literacy, familiarity with typing, communication abilities and fluency in English (Cowie, 2007; Ramesh, 2004; Taylor and Bain, 2005). Job positions could thus easily be filled with people having high school diplomas, and advanced training beyond that was not needed. It was the peculiarities of the Indian context that resulted in so many university graduates taking up employment in the ITES–BPO industry.

NASSCOM's Assessment of Competence (NAC) initiative, launched in 2006, addressed the issue of attrition. It operated as an industry standard assessment and certification programme to ensure the transformation of a 'trainable' workforce into an 'employable' workforce with a view to helping ITES–BPO employers reduce their hiring costs, improve efficiencies, enlarge the candidate pool and, perhaps more importantly, control the escalation of entry level wages. NAC, therefore, did not serve as a system of licensure (NASSCOM, 2007b).

Given the circumstances, call centre jobs did not fulfil the requisite belief that professional expertise was based on the performance of a vital function in society which required specialized knowledge and skill acquired through prolonged education and experience (Kornhauser, 1962). There was no legal or political position of privilege that protected call centre jobs from being encroached upon by other occupations. The functions of licensure, which provides a profession with a legal monopoly over the performance of some strategic aspect of its work and effectively prevents free competition from other occupations (Freidson, 1970), was not available to call centre agents. Moreover, in the wider job market, work experience in a mass customized call centre was not considered to be of much value even in related industries like IT. Therefore, it was a job that neither enhanced the status of employees nor promoted their careers in occupations where sound and specialized theoretical knowledge was required.

Professions are closely tied to the issue of autonomy which stems from the belief that qualified practitioners are best able to determine how the function ought to be performed and hence must be free to exercise their own judgment in specific cases (Kornhauser, 1962). The low levels of control associated with call centre jobs included in this book raises questions about autonomy. In fact, control was institutionalized through technology, strengthened and deepened by the use of bureaucratic controls in shaping the social and organizational structure of the workplace (Callaghan and Thompson, 2001).

Thus, as an occupational group, call centre agents are not able to be self-directing as they cannot control the production process, particularly the application of knowledge and skill in the work they perform. Moreover, the substance of their knowledge and skill was known to others—in this case, their superiors including the quality personnel, their clients and their customers—who could legitimately criticize and evaluate the way work was carried out.

Further, as Korczynski (2001) states, contemporaneously, the increasing importance accorded to customers entails a significant shift in the fabric of the employer organization from the uncontested dominance of the bureaucratic paradigm to the prevalence of a hybridization of bureaucracy and service orientation. Bureaucracy, representing a rational, efficient and routine authority, is combined with a customer focus, representing a more variable and unpredictable authority, resulting in the need for employee self-control while simultaneously fulfilling bureaucratic requirements. In the ensuing performance of emotional labour via remote mode in the context of technobureaucratic controls, call centre employees met the norm of professionalization as expressed by the degree to which work groups adhere to both the service ideal and professional conduct (Wilensky, 1964). However, the situation of call centre employees was far from Hughes's (1963) requirement that professionals seek to replace the usual stricture of caveat emptor (let the buyer beware) with the norm of credit emptor (let the buyer trust).

Instead of the customer acceding to the professional judgement of the call centre employee, the former appraised their own needs and judged the potential of the service provided to them. In other words, call centre agents could not profess to know better than their customers. On the contrary, the customer was able to evaluate the performance of the professional and was considered a true judge of the value of the service received. In fact, Indian call centre agents feared overseas customers suing the client which, in turn, would impact the business prospects of the Indian ITES–BPO sector and, subsequently, their own employment. Deference to customers, to the extent of altering cultural and linguistic orientation including adopting accents and pseudonyms and engaging in locational masking, predominated agents' jobs.

Going further, agents did not enjoy the authority vested in professionals, with customers expressing doubts over their competence and distrust over divulging personal and sensitive information. Cross-cultural factors complicated the situation. Under these circumstances, customers' insubordination to agents' professional authority divested them of the monopoly of judgment associated with a profession. This was contrary to Freidson's (1970) formulation that influence is not exerted by adducing persuasive evidence that professional advice is valid and, therefore, worth obeying. A professional's advice should be obeyed because it is a professional who gives it. Not surprisingly, Nanda (2005) put call centre agents outside the realm of those delineated as professionals. In his work, call centre agents relying on algorithm-based inference to provide services that are useful but not highly valued by customers, are not professionals.

Customers' claims of agents' incompetence and deceit have been buttressed by the fact that, every few months, there have been allegations appearing in the media that personal data of customers handled by Indian call centres were at risk. On all such occasions, NASSCOM has not only insisted that the perpetrators of these alleged frauds be brought to book but has also set up the National Skills Registry (NSR)—a centralized database of employees of the IT and ITES–BPO companies—to ensure that there is a verified database (with independent background checks) of the human resources present within the industry. The registration for the NSR touched the 125,000 mark as of July 2007 and NASSCOM's target was to take this number five times over to touch 500,000 by December 2007. This initiative, according to NASSCOM, would reduce the risk of appointing employees on the basis of fake/forged documents, lessen the cost and time involved in conducting background checks independently, facilitate faster completion of HR processes that depend on background checks, ensure customer information is in safe and secure hands, allow the Indian IT and ITES–BPO industry to confidently claim higher standards of recruitment practices and allow international customers to view employee information directly (NASSCOM, not dated b).

Besides, NASSCOM has been working very closely with Indian law enforcement organizations and has set up cyber training labs in

Mumbai, Thane, Pune and Bangalore to train police officers in cyber crime investigation. Further, the Data Security Council of India—a self-regulatory body for the Indian IT and ITES–BPO industry was set up in April 2007 to popularize, monitor and enforce privacy and data protection standards for India's IT and ITES–BPO industry (NASSCOM, not dated c and d). Thus, while there are no ethical codes governing the work ethos among call centre agents from within their own occupation as is the case with other professions, control is being imposed from outside. To elaborate, call centre agents have no governing body, composed of respected members of the profession, that oversees adherence to a code of conduct by establishing monitoring mechanisms, reviewing complaints and administering sanctions normally associated with professionals as a formal method of declaring to all that the occupation can be trusted and thereby of persuading society to grant the special status of autonomy.

In matters relating to the lifestyle of professionals, one aspect of Indian call centre agents' lives attest to the academic conceptualization. Self-immersion in one's work, reflecting personal involvement such that strain is absorbed and work-life imbalance is accepted (Greenwood, 1962) was visible, in keeping with the notion of professionalism that for a professional person, his/her work becomes his/her life (Greenwood, 1962).

Beyond this, however, the lifestyle associated with call centres does little to promote a professional image. The general opinion of call centres among the Indian public is that the young men and women working the phones at night constantly party and enjoy themselves, engaging in sex and drug-taking (*Khaleej Times Online*, 2006). Media reports suggest that call centre employees have come to acquire a reputation of having 'licentious lifestyles'(*The Sydney Morning Herald*, 2006), with stories of used condoms blocking call centre restroom drains and drug-taking during night shifts (Farrel, 2006). Some reports appearing in the press suggest that call centre staff have been caught by hidden cameras having sex in cubicles. Not only is such uninhibited conduct bewildering for middle class India (*The Sydney Morning Herald*, 2006), but also the Catholic Church in India has announced its intentions to address the problem of call centre promiscuity (Haines, 2006).

While many call centre agents included in this book maintained that these images, though not incorrect, were exaggerated, older agents were unforgiving in their comments. According to them, the young workforce joining the industry was uncouth, uncultured, casual, irresponsible, carefree and extravagant. Call centre agents saw too much of money and freedom at a young age, both of which they were unable to handle. The money they earned was considered to be pocket money which they spent on excessive drinking, partying, dating, smoking and living lavishly. Overspending, rather than saving, was the norm. Older agents rued the overemphasis on unfavourable Western practices creeping into Indian society, wishing that Indian youth would emulate positive Western values. Older agents pointed out that from the moment young people took up jobs in the call centres, parents lost control. Young agents often lied to their parents about working on night shifts, when they are actually partying with friends. Moreover, older agents were aghast with the overemphasized collegial organizational culture and the lack of respect shown to the superiors which, in their view, stemmed from the independence agents had achieved vis-à-vis their parents.

> People have this negative view about call centres. Lot of my friends say that I am in a bad industry. Call centres have this reputation about themselves—there are only parties and one is always having a good time—ITES–BPO industry has somewhat created a scandal.
>
> You can call me as an 80's guy. I am not a 90's guy. If I am given a chance to have a holiday, I will sit at home. I am not a kind of guy who goes for parties, who goes out at nights, I don't believe in that. In a way, the younger generation has lot of money in their hands. They don't know how to spend it properly. They have no controls. Sometimes you feel sorry for them. I have seen girls, 20 and 21 years old, who had abortions. Parents don't know about it. Boozing and all goes on. Fifteen or 20 years back, if you had a BCom or BA, you could hardly get a job. But now, you get a job and the kind of salary you get—your dad won't have earned that much in his career. That is the positive side. But the flip side is they have too much and there is no control. Especially during the weekends, the girls will switch cabs. The transport policy clearly states that a lady should be picked up from her doorstep and drop at doorstep. But during the weekends, they want to go somewhere else. I have brought that to the management's notice and they were like, 'What's your problem? They are all grown ups'.[1]

---

[1] Participant quotes are included in this chapter to illustrate the various themes. For reasons of confidentiality, participants have not been identified individually.

Undoubtedly, this public image of call centre employees, coupled with a lack of expertise, authority and autonomy, stringent monitoring, customer control and the absence of a code of conduct, does not compare with the image building activity that occupations require to pursue in order that the public recognizes the occupation to be a profession (Forsyth and Danisiewicz, 1985). The image-building activity requires professionals to display the service as essential, exclusive and complex to the public, with successful public recognition resulting in the award of autonomy. The ambivalence with which call centre agents are regarded perhaps further complicates matters. To quote Cowie (2007):

> ...the way that these new workers are described in the English language broadsheets such as *Times of India* or *Asian Age* is ambivalent. On the one hand, they are the cool new generation, symbolic of India's economic growth, who have 'work hard play hard' lifestyles and are financially independent. On the other hand, they are 'cyber coolies' who are 'not in a real job'.

Managerial Insights

Findings emerging from the analysis of call centre managers' interview data highlighted the discrepancy between the conceptualization of professionalism as communicated to employees and the enactment of professionalism within the employer organization. As pointed out earlier, call centre organizations cultivated the notion of professionalism in employees through induction training, on-going socialization, performance evaluation mechanisms and other elements of organizational design, in order to gain their compliance and commitment to the fulfilment of the organizations' goals. Organizations banked on agents' internalization of the professional identity to meet client requirements and SLAs and thereby retain their competitive positions. While employer organizations maintained that the notion of professionalism defined their culture, using both material and processual evidence to back up their position, in reality, where their agents are concerned, they did not completely deliver on all their claims of the espousal of professionalism, as managerial data show. Through the themes of informality and non-hierarchical structures, career growth, workplace ambience and transparency described further, managers' acknowledgement of this duality is illustrated. Managers' interviews also show that their sense of discomfort with this discrepancy is overshadowed by their allegiance to organizational effectiveness, which they see as critical to organizational survival and to the continuity of employment for all those associated with the organization, including themselves. Apparently, then, for employer organizations, as far as their agents go, the notion of professionalism is relevant more as a means of identity regulation within the framework of socio-ideological control to achieve the organizational agenda. Beyond this instrumentalism, in matters linked to agents, organizations do not display much concern about further engagement with the notion of professionalism.

Informality and Non-hierarchical Structures

Employer organizations, in communications to agents, downplayed bureaucratic structures and processes and emphasized integration. This orientation was particularly associated with superior–subordinate interactions and grievance handling processes. Agents were made to believe that a respectful informality characterized their relationships with superiors, being reinforced by the collegial atmosphere at work. Further, agents were given to understand that they were free to approach any superior in the organization to redress their problems. On both these counts, references to the organization's professional orientation, value for employees and espousal of progressive aspects of Western culture were made.

In reality, managers expressed discomfort with agents' informal though deferential behaviour with them. They resented being addressed by their first names and being treated as equals, even though this coexisted with respect. Managers responded to such display of informality either by unfairly picking on agents or by sidelining and ignoring them. Contrary to the discourse on integration and irrelevance of hierarchy that they themselves had propagated to the agents, managers expected agents to maintain traditional bureaucratic symbols within the organization and hence appreciated older agents who displayed appropriate restraint.

Similarly, managers expected agents to follow the due process of grievance handling. Agents' reliance on the much publicized open door policy and skip-level meeting practice invited victimization, which was sometimes so severe and prolonged that it left the concerned agents with no choice but to quit the organization (Noronha and D'Cruz, 2008b). Indeed, managers viewed agents' use of these policies with a sense of threat and suspicion. In their view, agents were either challenging them or holding them to ransom. Not only was such behaviour interpreted as unprofessional and immature and as indicative of wrong attitudes, but the managerial response to it emerged in the form of a nexus which, in protecting this group's collective and individual interests, victimized agents. Undoubtedly, in contrast to what was espoused, employers' openness to feedback and commitment to employee well-being were questionable, confirming the Budhwar et al.'s (2006) observation that management mostly acted as a closed system.

> Sometimes, without telling the immediate manager, they just walk out to the HR and start talking, which is not the right thing to do. So we will say, 'Listen, there is a definite procedure to escalate these problems.'

> An open door policy is that you can skip a level of management and talk to the next level. Again, these issues should not go against your current boss. Otherwise, it will not work well for an agent. That is seen as challenging the authority of the manager.

Compounding the rhetoric of informality and non-hierarchical structures in call centre organizations were the interactive effects of age and position. For instance, older agents joining the industry did not appreciate younger TLs' and managers' behaviour towards them. They believed that they should be treated respectfully by colleagues young enough to be their offspring. Likewise, promotions of younger agents to managerial positions were seen as allowing arrogance, immaturity and inexperience to permeate organizational functioning.

Career Growth

Employer organizations' promises about career growth, made at the time of recruitment and followed up by various announcements and initiatives during agents' tenure, included promotion opportunities at quick rates and promotion criteria of objectivity and merit linked to performance.

Managerial interviews highlighted caveats on both these counts. Though promotion opportunities for agents existed and were implemented with regular periodicity, the opportunities themselves were limited in number and scope, given the peculiarities of organizational structure, as previously shown by Budhwar et al. (2006). Indeed, competition for the TL position was intense, given the limited number of posts and the large number of applicants, since the bottom-heavy, flat structure of call centres automatically restricted the number of promotion openings available to agents. As Batt et al. (2005a) earlier found, to compensate and give the impression of providing growth, organizations engaged in horizontal/lateral growth strategies which entailed job enlargement combined with minimal job enrichment and hierarchical movement. In this manner, more layers were added to the agent level with new designations that indicated a move away from being only an agent but did not signify entry into the TL position which was the lowest level supervisory job. In that sense, movement was illusory. While agents seeking career growth valued the limited vertical movement afforded by such initiatives, considering these to be stepping stones to supervisory positions, they were disappointed with the long wait involved in moving into the TL level. At the same time, given the number of agents vis-à-vis the number of positions, even these incremental promotion initiatives did not guarantee growth to all agents.

> I will tell you...earlier, in the operational division, there were agents, team leaders, team managers and vice presidents (VPs). That is it. Today, there are trainee CSRs, CSRs, senior CSRs, TCs, TLs, project leaders, assistant managers, manager-operations, senior managers and VPs. In many organizations, senior CSRs and TCs are same while the only difference between the position of project leader and TL is the size of the teams.

> In the industry, they created a post called subject matter expert. Why? It is nothing but lateral growth and horizontal growth. It is very misleading. Okay, I am going to show a carrot and say, 'Hey, listen! This is what you're going to get.' Create another post. What is the firm trying to achieve out of this?

While objective performance data were consulted, subjectivity played a role in promotion decisions, operating in three ways. First, a long list of attributes such as being out-going, mature, motivated, target-oriented, customer-oriented, possessitng good communication and social skills, accepting additional responsibilities, displaying openness to feedback, being a team player, exhibiting leadership qualities, respecting superiors and striving for perfection was considered important. However, interpretations of and emphasis given to such behaviour in agents varied across supervisors. Second, the influence of ethnic factors, in particular religion, region and caste, was clear, as previously highlighted by Noronha (2005) in the context of Indian industry. Third, agents' visibility in the organization, determined by his/her enacted commitment to the organization, extra-role initiatives on the job and relationships with superiors, was significant.

Adhering to organizational requirements and absorbing work-related strain, without complaining, was considered to be a measure of employee commitment. Apart from acceptance of technobureaucratic controls and deference to customers, this translated into extending work days and work weeks, shortening or forfeiting breaks, foregoing holidays and leave even in instances of illness and favouring organizational leisure activities over personal engagements even on weekly and public holidays. The perceived commitment of an agent determined the nature of and knowledge about his/her image within the organization.

Agents were judged on the basis of voluntary initiatives, beyond their jobs. These initiatives could relate to undertaking team-building activities, sharing best practices, generating new ideas, filling in for TLs, working beyond shift timings, preparing reports for superiors, conducting in-house courses, helping to reduce attrition, managing the shift, satisfying clients and displaying managerial qualities such as accountability and integrity.

But cultivating a network of superiors was by far the most critical factor. Most of our managerial participants confirmed that being in the superior's 'good books' was essential for a promotion. They described instances of agents attempting to win over superiors through interactions within and outside the office and then subsequently convincing them of the suitability of their candidature. Such interactions took various forms including doing favours for, carrying tales to and spying on others on behalf of the managers. In addition, male managers in our study stated that women agents either voluntarily or involuntarily got into relationships with male managers. According to them, good-looking women had an undue advantage in getting ahead by dressing 'provocatively' and dating their male bosses. While women managers in our study agreed that this was true in some instances, they cited numerous promotions whose basis did not revolve around gender though other aspects of subjectivity may have been present.

Managers highlighted that under such circumstances where agents' networks carried credence, not only were undeserving candidates promoted but also one could predict who the successful candidate would be even prior to the selection process. Such a situation reinforces Budhwar et al.'s (2006) finding that favouritism played a role in appraisal and promotion processes in Indian call centres. Phrases such as 'buttering', 'bootlicking' and 'apple polishing', widely used in Indian organizations (See Noronha, 2005), are commonly referred to in the Indian call centre industry.

Managers attributed the aforementioned emergence of subjectivity to the rapid growth of the ITES–BPO industry which has allowed people with low levels of skill and talent to occupy key positions. Further, norms of grooming and nurturing future leaders provide superiors with enough scope to pick incapable people whom they like or who do not threaten their own positions. At times, the need to meet targets results in denying promotions to outstanding agents while allowing poorly performing agents to move ahead.

While some agents are able to manage these complex circumstances and advance their careers, there are numerous other agents who are either unsuccessful or experience slower rates of growth. It is in these latter instances that we see the rhetoric associated with career growth fuelling organizational attrition. That is, as these agents realized that their vertical movement was constrained by organizational design elements and by subjective evaluation processes, they sought to further their career growth by moving to other organizations within the ITES–BPO sector. Even though the situation was no different in other organizations, agents failed to realize it at first, being taken in by the fresh start they were making. They maintained that they had been deceived by their previous employer but were now valued by their new employer who could be counted on to deliver on stated promises. Managerial data point out how agents once again get convinced by organizational claims about career growth, only to realize later that they have fallen prey to their earlier predicament. It is only after some passage of time in the new organization that they realize that the circumstances surrounding promotions here are no different compared to those in their previous organization.

Managers were quick to highlight that the limitations placed on career growth, as described earlier, were the primary reasons behind the much-publicized attrition present in this sector. They emphasized that attrition involved movement from one organization to another within this sector, and not movement from this sector to another one. In their view, the material gains associated with jobs in this sector were responsible for agents' continued presence here.

It is relevant to describe, in brief, the experiences of women managers in the Indian call centre industry. While women managers included in our study asserted that their promotions were purely merit-based, they underscored the gender-based hostility they experienced in supervisory and managerial positions. They elaborated that as agents, gender had no relevance for them, but became important with vertical movement, reflecting Singh and Pandey's (2005) observation. Women managers recounted that they were often not taken seriously, having to put in extra effort to prove themselves. Often, their ideas were not accepted and their decisions were criticized and ignored. Further, they were often subject to derogatory comments and chauvinistic jokes. The prevalence of a glass ceiling in the industry cannot be denied.

> When you give some ideas or suggestions, they will say, 'Okay, that's a very good idea, no problem.' But they stop it there. You can understand that from their tone of voice.

Women managers also faced resistance from their male subordinates. Besides, night shifts and domestic responsibilities added to their challenges, given the social context. McMillin's (2006), Ng and Mitter's (2005), Ramesh's (2004) and Singh and Pandey's (2005) findings are thus reinforced.

> Sometimes the male ego comes in between. Then you have to tell them, 'Hey, you know what, I am the boss, and you have to listen to me.' I speak in that way. Initially, I used to feel bad. I wish I had been a man, things might have been a lot easier.

Workplace Ambience

While agents described the workplace ambience of call centres in terms of employer concern for employee well-being, nested within both the professional orientation and the issue of work-life balance, managers shed light on the underlying intentions.

According to managers, the only thing that mattered to employer organizations was meeting client requirements and SLAs in order to maintain competitive advantage. Workplace ambience was relevant only within this context. This is in line with Ramesh's (2004) observation that work and fun are balanced to create a productively docile workforce and that employers' espoused commitment to employee interests is eclipsed by the primacy of the management, giving agents an illusionary sense of freedom and flexibility.

Elaborating further, managers pointed out that while the collegial atmosphere of the organization was promoted to energize and destress employees so that they could relate to the workplace and their performance could be maximized, fun initiatives held during work days were scheduled such that they never interfered with task requirements. Usually, fun activities were held either during breaks or before or after the shift. During the shift, such activities were held only when call volumes were low.

Similar programmes during weekly and public or festival holidays were conducted with several purposes in mind. While such activities formed part of the identity regulation-socio-ideological control programme, they were means of understanding employees better and using this information to organizational advantage, of assessing employees' commitment to work and to the employer organization and working towards strengthening this and of facilitating team development. Though organizations were aware that the team bonding emerging from such activities could be the starting point for collectivization and resistance, they worked to ensure that the attachment between team members served organizational purposes. References to the transactional psychological contract of employment were used to keep collectivist resistance at bay. Managers stated that in their view, engaging agents during holidays ensured that they got little spare time in which to indulge in any activity that interfered with their fulfilment of work requirements but remained within team, process and organizational boundaries. Though team bonding worked in a positive way, managers admitted that its one adverse effect was its influence on attrition, that is, if one member of a team quit the organization, it was not uncommon for other members to follow suit.

> It (fun activities held outside the office on holidays) is useful. Lot of people would not open up in the office. May be a drink or a soft drink would open them up. If the inhibitions are shed, inside or outside office, you can gel better, you can communicate better. You can put your thoughts across in a much simpler manner.

As has also been observed by Ng and Mitter (2005), quite often the latter set of programmes involved agents' families as well, the objective being to gain family loyalty to the organization so that, indirectly, agents' commitment could be strengthened, their performance could be improved and the chances of attrition could be stalled. Managers described the reactions of parents of call centre agents from middle, lower middle and lower-class families to such events. Given their exposure, lifestyle and aspirations, these parents were stupefied with the material artefacts associated with the employer organization. Being a part of the planned leisure programme, they also believed that the organization was concerned about employees' well-being. Realizing that their offspring's employment with such progressive and generous organizations had altered their standard of living, parents developed a sense of awe of and loyalty towards the organization. Parents' sentiments operated as restraining factors in agents' decisions about their continuity of employment with the organisation, though parents were not always completely successful in the long run because of agents' concern with career growth issues.

Participation in organizational leisure activities planned on weekly and public holidays was considered to be a measure of agent commitment and played an important role in decisions about agents' career growth. Managers pointed out that under such circumstances, call centre agents felt compelled to attend these programmes. They elaborated that many agents would prefer to spend their spare time as they wished but felt unable to exercise this choice. The situation appears to reflect Spicer and Fleming's (2004) stand that culture management was used to push the inside sphere of corporate culture out into other aspects of employees' lives.

Undoubtedly, workplace ambience was a means of facilitating the fulfilment of the organization's agenda and was never accorded priority over organizational requirements.

> At the end of the day, you need to work. Fun and games are a cover up for the hard work and cutting costs.

Managers' interviews revealed that so great was the organizations' preoccupation with the completion of SLAs that they work out figures greater than those specified by clients and hand these to agents to deliver. While it was quite clear that employer organizations did not want to take any risks with clients, using such a means as a buffer, these practices caused strain for agents. Not only could employer organizations hold clients responsible for the stringent parameters expected of agents, linking this to process continuity and renewal, organizational survival and employment opportunities, but organizations also denied agents access to the organization–client SLA document, citing reasons of protocol.

> When I became the manager, I realized that the SLAs given to agents are higher than those agreed to by the clients. This is done to make sure that we achieve the client's targets. For example, when my client gives an SLA of 60, I give my agent 70, so that we achieve the target.

Operational excellence agendas being currently adopted in the Indian ITES–BPO sector in order to sustain the long-term viability of India's cost advantage in global offshoring (NASSCOM, 2006) only further employer organizations' emphasis on performance parameters, turning workplace ambience into a rhetoric. Managers spoke of cost cutting measures resulting in limits on recruitment such that agents had to extend work days and work weeks in order to meet higher target levels. Managers acknowledged that such developments have adverse implications for agents' performance and well-being. But they admitted that unless agents' performance deteriorated, nothing was done to address the situation and agents were sometimes working 6 to 7 days a week without a weekly holiday for 2 to 3 weeks. Managers expressed helplessness over the situation, pointing out that their failure to adhere to organizational requirements would cost them their jobs. In their view, top management, in its focus on costs, was losing its humanistic perspective.

> Let's say a simple thing. There are times where there is shortage of agents. So at that time, we ask the existing agents to stretch, they will oblige for 2–3 weeks, beyond that it is difficult. Obviously, the performance will deteriorate if they work without offs. However, senior management says that recruiting more people doesn't arise since it's just a seasonal

wave—X'mas or Easter time. Top management looks for numbers and has lost its personal touch.

The foregoing description of task-related demands explains why recreational and leisure facilities and educational opportunities provided by employer organizations become redundant. Agents had absolutely no time to take advantage of them. The little spare time they enjoyed was allocated to sleep, family and friends and personal chores.

> Since ICFAI University is having tie-ups with our organization, they are coming up with various courses—but I am not able to squeeze out much time for it. It again depends on my shift timings, I have my own schedules and all. As of now, it is not possible for me.

Managerial data leave no doubt that employee well-being, packaged in the garb of workplace ambience, occupies a secondary position, being completely overshadowed by the organization's preoccupation with competitive advantage. Indeed, workplace ambience is a mere means to this end. To borrow from Legge (2006) and Storey (1993), a hard HRM model is being couched in soft terms.

Transparency

Managers' interviews highlighted the absence of transparency in various aspects of employer organizations' functioning that interfaced with agents' lives.

> Transparency is certainly talked about in most situations. They talk about walking the talk, leading from the front...but I seldom see people here sticking to it. It takes a real principle-oriented person to deliver on transparency and it becomes hard when the ambience and circumstances are not helpful.

Managers indicated that at the time of recruiting potential employees, organizations do not clarify the specific nature of work to be undertaken by them. At this stage, candidates are given the impression that they are being screened by an MNC organization. It is only after actually joining the organization, at the time of induction training, that employees realize that they would be working as call centre agents.

But most of them choose to continue with employment here because it remains the best option available to them.

Another area where a lack of transparency is apparent is that of agents' remuneration. It is a common practice, at the time of recruitment, to disclose remuneration to agents in terms of cost-to-company (CTC). While CTC is the total amount of expenditure an organization undertakes for an employee in a particular year, including gross pay, variable pay, long-term benefits, leave travel allowance, medical reimbursement, transport, food, other allowances and loyalty bonus, this figure does not translate into the monthly salary that agents receive which is a much lower amount. However, agents, most of whom are freshers entering the job market for the first time, do not realize that this is the case until they receive their first salary. Nonetheless, even at this juncture, agents believe not only that their returns are much better than what they would receive in other sectors but also that numerous other components of the CTC which do not form part of their salary accrue to them in some form and represent employers' investment in them. While agents thus remain happy in spite of the discrepancy, managers maintain that their experience on this count points out to the absence of transparency.

Managers elaborated how the basis for agents' promotions remained unclear to them. Though employer organizations cited objectivity and merit linked to performance as the determinants of promotions, various other factors, as delineated in the theme on career growth, influenced the process. Agents, going by organizations' specified criteria, were baffled by promotion decisions which were not in keeping with stated norms. Attempting to understand the rationale behind these decisions, some agents would make inquiries with their superiors or with the HR department. Superiors' and HR managers' responses, which appeared to be unrelated to the specified criteria, allowed vagueness to surround the issue of promotion. Managers provided illustrations of these replies: mismatch of skills, mismatch between personal objectives and organization goals, failure to meet business objectives, inability to be an effective team player, contribution limited to the scope of work, lack of preparedness for the next level, suitability at current position not a predictor of appropriateness for the next level, excellence in performance not an indicator of leadership potential, and strengths in current performance a reinforcer for continuity at the present position. Managers pointed out that superiors' and HR managers' creation of such haziness furthered agents' confusion as to what constituted the real determinants of career growth.

The issue of process status was similarly handled. Employer organizations never divulged the truth about process termination, process continuity and process renewal, even when agents sought confirmation of circulating rumours. Further on the same lines, as discussed earlier, SLAs as jointly agreed upon by the client and the employer organization were never shared with agents. On the contrary, targets higher than those specified in the SLA document were given to agents in order to guard against any risk of the organization's failure to deliver and subsequent withdrawal of the process by the client.

According to managers included in our study, agents' professional identity (inculcated and nurtured by the organization's identity regulation-socio-ideological control initiative) coupled with the privilege accorded to transactional psychological contracts in the ITES–BPO industry as well as lack of other attractive employment options in the Indian context facilitates the organization's limited engagement with transparency in matters concerning agents.

7

Final Word

The lived experience of call centre agents included in our study was captured by the core theme of being professional. The notion of professionalism embraced agents' identity, altering their self-concept and enhancing their self-esteem. According to agents, professionals possess superior cognitive abilities, advanced qualifications and a sense of responsibility and commitment to work. They prioritize work over personal needs and pleasure, behaving in a dignified and restrained manner and performing optimally and rationally while on the job. Professionals comply with job and organizational requirements, absorbing emergent strain. Under such circumstances, not only do agents perceive gains accruing from their job as consistent with the notion of professionalism but also transactional psychological contracts of employment as means of discipline are similarly justified. Though resistance is displayed by some agents a few times, this is described as a temporary outlet to ease job-related strain, coexisting with professional identity—it is not an indicator of anti-work or anti-employer sentiment. Indeed, agents' professional identity precludes engagement with collectivization attempts which are seen both as inconsistent with the essential features of professionalism and as redundant in instances where employers protect employee interests.

Through agents' narratives, the context surrounding their professional identity came out vividly. Organizations cultivated the notion of professionalism in employees through induction training, on-going socialization, performance evaluation mechanisms and other elements of organizational design, with a view to gain their compliance and commitment to the realization of the organization's agenda.

That professional identity is greatly valued as a symbol of social status and upward mobility in the Indian context facilitated the process. Indeed, professional identity allowed agents to accept task and organizational demands in spite of the strain they engendered. Material artefacts and organizational processes were cited as proof of the organization's espousal of professionalism. Though, in reality, organizations did not fully deliver on their claims relating to the latter, professed commitment to employee well-being, rooted in the notion of professionalism, served organizational interests in maintaining a conducive intra-organizational and extra-organizational environment that allowed business to flourish (see Chapter 4 of this book).

The cultivation of professional identity in agents and its subsequent internalization and influence on agents reflects the identity regulation processes present in employer organizations. Identity regulation, which refers to discursive practices concerned with identity definition that condition processes of identity formation and transformation (Alvesson and Willmott, 2002), encompasses the idea that individual identity can be altered and managed. It is rooted in the notion of self-pluralism which highlights the temporal and situational changeability and constancy of identity (McReynolds et al., 2000). In other words, while individual identity can remain constant over setting and time, it can also change, sometimes drastically, across context and time. Drawing on this premise, organizations espouse the position and adopt the agenda of regulating and managing the identity of their members as part of the organizational control process.

Organizational control stems from the need to contain the divergent interests of individual employees and prevent them from interfering with organizational goals. That is, organizations seek mechanisms to circumscribe employees' idiosyncratic behaviours and ensure conformity such that employee self-interests and disruptions are minimized and organizational objectives are served (Hatch and Cunliffe, 2006). The most potent manner in which such control is executed is via identity regulation (Alvesson and Willmott, 2002), whereby organizations seek to shape the subjectivity of their employees (Knights and Morgan, 1991), with a view to ensuring organizational effectiveness.

In the present study, identity regulation operated via the notion of professionalism (it is relevant to highlight at this juncture that Ramesh [2004] also mentions the presence of professionalism in the

Indian call centre industry though he does not explore its character and complexity). The professions are singled out as occupations that perform tasks of great social value because those enacting them possess knowledge and skill that in some way set them apart from other kinds of workers, in addition to being subject to a self-regulating form of social control (Freidson, 1984). Professionals include those who perform the tasks associated with the professions and are considered to be distinctive because of the special attitude and concern they bring to their work (Freidson, 1984). Professional, therefore, refers to not only people enacting the profession but also to the characteristics expected of the members of specific professions (Middlehurst and Kennie, 1999). Cast as a means of control with concomitant performance, accountability and commitment, professionalism is considered to have distinct advantages for professionals, employers and customers in terms of facilitating the provision of superior service (Evetts, 2003; Freidson, 2001).

Evetts (2003) points out the growing appeal of the ideas of profession, professional and professionalism and their increased use in all work contexts. It is an attractive prospect for an occupation to be considered a profession and for occupational workers to be identified as professionals, resulting in the proliferation of the discourse of professionalism in organizational contexts. Indeed, the terms profession, professional and professionalism are commonly used in organizational mission statements, aims and objectives to motivate and mystify employees, thereby serving as disciplinary and control mechanisms for governing employees from a distance.

Fournier (1999: 290) has demonstrated how the reconstitution of employees as professionals involves more than just a process of re-labelling '...it also involves the delineation of "appropriate work identities" and potentially allows for control at a distance by inscribing the disciplinary logic of professionalism within the person of the employee so labelled'. Fournier's (1999) argument applies to the Indian call centre industry as well—that is, employers' use of the professional identity in the case of call centre agents does not only constitute a mere re-labelling invoked as a means of keeping the agents outside the purview of the Industrial Disputes Act, 1947 (Banerjee, 2006), but the appeal to professionalism also operates with the realm of organizational control processes. Both in new and existing occupational and organizational contexts, employees are expected to recast themselves as professionals who are self-controlled and self-motivated to perform in ways that the organization defines as appropriate (Fournier, 1999). It calls for the alignment of professional conduct and competence with personal orientation and development. Those who master the discourse of professionalism and perform in ways the organization defines as desirable are rewarded with career promotion and progress (Evetts, 2003; Fournier, 1999).

Evetts (2003) reinforces this argument, highlighting that while employees are very keen to grasp and lay claim to the normative values of and multiple benefits associated with professionalism, in effect, professionalism is being used as an ideology and a discourse to convince, cajole and persuade employees to perform and behave in ways which the organization deems to be appropriate, effective and efficient (Evetts, 2003).

Identity regulation forms part of organizations' socio-ideological control (alternatively termed as cultural/normative control) process, which targets values, ideas, beliefs, emotions and identification of employees (Alvesson, 2001) and where control is accomplished through the self-positioning of employees within managerially inspired discourses about work and organization with which they become identified and committed (Alvesson and Willmott, 2002). Indeed, the controls of today's corporation are infinitely subtler, reaching to the very core of each employee's sense of selfhood and identity, defining his/her very being (Gabriel 1999). As Deetz (1995) maintains, the attempt is to manage employee cognitions and emotions rather than only their behaviours. Such programmes seek to promote an ethos that demands loyalty from employees and that excludes, silences or punishes those who question its creed. In this manner, the space within organizations for expressing and developing awareness of, and allegiance to, alternative norms or values is reduced and, ideally, eliminated. People willingly perform jobs because their sense of purpose and identity is tightly coupled to the core values of the corporation (Willmott, 1993).

Most current literature establishes that socio-ideological controls are primary controls in their own right, complementing and reinforcing other bureaucratic and technological controls, which reside in organizational structure, manufacturing processes and surveillance mechanisms (Gabriel, 1999). Yet, the relationship between traditional bureaucratic, technological and socio-ideological forms of control appears to be complex. Instead of a clear-cut, simple and mechanical explanation (as represented by an algorithm), the interplay between different forms of controls reflects a social process (van Maanen and Kunda, 1989). These different techniques are not necessarily independent but overlap with one another (Fournier, 1999), as the study findings highlight. That is, socio-ideological forms of control, demonstrated in the present study through identity regulation via the notion of being professional, pave the way for the acceptance of strict technobureacratic forms of control. van Maanen and Kunda (1989) observe that socio-ideological controls interface with, rather than substitute, other forms of control. Undoubtedly, instead of a discontinuity, socio-ideological controls set the stage for the effectiveness of technological controls, resulting in a hybridization of the various forms of control. This enables us to go beyond Fournier's (1999) formulation that the notion of professionalism as a disciplinary mechanism is not only being extended to new occupational domains where employees' behaviour cannot be regulated through direct control but is also being relied upon in organizations where employees are closely monitored, such as in call centres. Socio-ideological and technobureaucratic forms of control clearly build on and feed each other (Alvesson and Karreman, 2004).

That call centre agents, in spite of their professional identity and the presence of transactional psychological contracts, devise means of overcoming technobureaucratic controls in order to manage work-related strain points out the gaps in the organizational control process. Though agents maintain that their commitment to the notion of professionalism remains intact, the question as to whether the disciplinary logic of professionalism, combined with technobureaucratic controls, is an imperfect form of governance raises itself.

Agents' professional identity complicates collectivization endeavours, as has been highlighted in Chapter 5. Little has been published on union activity in call centres (Bain and Taylor, 2002), with most of the available literature focusing on organizational barriers to union recruitment. Earlier research shows that the intensive and individualistic nature of the work, the inability to interact with colleagues or leave work stations, the job design, the high turnover of call centre employees, complex and variable shift patterns (Bain and Taylor, 2001 and 2002), management control strategies such as close monitoring (Todd et al., 2003) and blacklisting those with union backgrounds or previously working in highly unionized firms (van den Broek, 2003) have made it difficult for unions to gain a footing within call centres. Nonetheless, Bain and Taylor (2001) maintain that although these barriers to union recruitment and organization are formidable, they are far from insuperable (Bain and Taylor, 2001), with call centre agents being capable of individual and collective resistance (Taylor and Bain, 1999). Though DeCotiis and Le Louarn (1981) would argue that unfair treatment and dissatisfaction with terms and conditions of employment are enough reason for unionization, Taylor and Bain (2003c) assert that extreme work conditions such as those present in call centres may not provide a sufficient push into union organization and recognition and the emergence and cultivation of workplace leaders would seem to hold the key to call centre unionization (Bain et al., 2004).

Yet, as in most debates on union formation, the identity dimensions of unionization have also been largely ignored (Milton, 2003) in call centre literature. Indeed, viewing unionization simply as a response to dissatisfaction and adversity masks the complexities of both the effect of identity on the propensity of employees to unionize and the role that unionization plays in employee identity (Milton, 2003). Our work has highlighted how call centre agents' professional identity complicates the process of collectivization, triggering changes in the approaches that trade unions and labour activists must employ. As Chapter 5 has shown, the strategies relevant to organizing call centre employees in India's ITES–BPO sector revolved around the issue of the professional identity acquired by them. Joining a union was seen as being inappropriate to the status of the international facing call centre employee and as rejecting key professional values. Moreover, poor public opinion of trade unions, employers' use of fear and conflict and the propagation by employers of providing good organization processes further deterred agents. While these factors resulted in agents' apathetic attitude towards unions, it was the intervention of union leaders from various sectors of the Indian economy and from international unions that initiated the collectivization process in the Indian ITES–BPO sector. Partnership was envisaged as the only possibility to create a new union identity that would be acceptable to ITES–BPO employees and to employer organizations. This did not mean co-optation of the union by employers but responsible unionism given the environment in which the union functioned. The key to current union enthusiasm for partnership reflected not the advance or defence of members' interests as such but the opportunity partnership agreements present to restate the legitimacy of trade union presence and to reinforce its organizational underpinnings in workplaces. Combining the role of a traditional union with that of a professional association paves the way forward. Clearly, there is potential in unions embracing certain practices of professional associations as part of an effort to lay the foundation for eventual unionization (Hurd, 2000).

It is relevant to mention that the move to link professional associations and unions adds to the ongoing debate within the related literature. On the one hand, the most commonly held view on the relationship of professionals with unions is that professionals do not require unions as professional associations already exist to advance the cause of the professions; unions are viewed as protecting the less capable, compressing salary differences and compromising highest standards and merit-based practices. Professionals have opposed unions because they think unions are incompatible with professional status (Kornhauser, 1962). Moreover, if professionals become infatuated with the need to fight for their own economic rights it would entail a rejection of key professional values leading to de-professionalization of the occupation (Raelin, 1989). The use of coercive union tactics to advance the cause of professionals only undermines the public image of the profession, equating them to factory hands (Faia, 1976). Thus, as Seidman and Cain (1964) argue, the professionals' lofty social status is likely to work against their joining ranks with other occupations or using tactics that are identified with working class unionism. In the context of call centre agents, though the role of an association is limited, the reasons for opting in favour of it are similar to those just delineated.

On the other hand, contrary to the above view, contemporary research argues that a growing number of professionals have turned to unionization in their efforts to enhance or preserve their professional prerogatives (Harrison, 1994). Rabban (1991) states that unionization and professionalism are not inherently incompatible. In fact, unionization is related to the profession's deteriorating market position or attempts which resist the imposition of bureaucratic constraints

(Raelin, 1989). Therefore, Rabban (1991) asserts that unionization does not lead to de-professionalization, but de-professionalization occurs first and the emerging union attempts to stop any further deterioration of the professionals' power base and/or to preserve and enhance their professional prerogatives. Thus, strikers desire more autonomy, authority and control in the workplace and are more professionally oriented than non-strikers (Falk et al., 1982). In effect, unionization can promote the cause of the profession by demonstrating to its employers as well as to a more informed public that a professional group can concomitantly meet public obligations while securing its own civil liberties (Raelin, 1989) and militancy is not motivated primarily by narrow self-interest but works towards the benefit of the larger society (Jessup, 1978). Going further, Rabban (1991) points out that even traditional unions now emphasize that collective bargaining can and should address distinctively professional concerns. Correspondingly, many professional associations have shifted from the view that collective bargaining is unprofessional, espousing such means to achieve professional goals. Pro-union sympathizers among professionals tend to be more professional than union antagonists, experiencing both relative dissatisfaction and powerlessness in their jobs and the desire for greater authority to govern their work activities (Raelin, 1989).

It is possible that, in reality, both the above perspectives may operate in a complex cohesion rather than as black-and-white categories, posing real dilemmas to the professionals themselves and to the organizations that represent them. On one hand, professionals look at unions as institutions better suited to blue-collar occupations and low wage service work, while on the other hand, professionals who feel that they are not given the respect they deserve join together in an association or a union. This equivocal stance of professionals towards union's results in tensions between union objectives related to terms and conditions of employment and professional objectives related to standards, ethics and customer needs. Thus, professionals struggle with the question of how to reconcile unionism with professionalism (Hurd, 2000).

It is pertinent to keep in mind that the choice of professionals to unionize is contingent on environmental and workplace conditions that create pressures or opportunities to do so. Similarly, union activity depends on the group's capacity to mobilize for effective union action which, in turn, depends on the availability of resources, leadership skills and communication networks, on interactions and emergent behaviour among members as well as on contextual factors (Harrison, 1994).

The taxonomic and power approaches from the sociology of professions illuminate the paradox engendered in engaging the term 'professional' to describe call centre agents. Undoubtedly, work systems and job design elements associated with the mass customized model of India's international facing call centres keep their agents out of the purview of the professional service model (Batt and Moynihan, 2002). Nonetheless, the rhetoric of high commitment management practices (Kinnie et al., 2000) adopted by these organizations coalesced to define call centre agents' identity as that of being professional. Managerial data underscore how the rhetoric of professionalism enabled employer organizations to use language to construct instrumental discourses aimed at altering agents' cognitions, emotions and behaviours (Hamilton, 2001; Watson, 2003). Though this construction of professional identity was a deliberate attempt on the part of employer organizations to gain employee compliance and commitment to the organizational agenda (Fournier, 1999), agents' narratives demonstrate that control was not totalizing.

Insights gained from call centre managers establish that the rhetoric of professionalism is indeed a false claim (Sisson, 1994; Storey, 2001), concerned only with impressing and misleading agents. In fact, as Storey (2001) asserts, the rhetoric adopted by employer organizations frequently embraces the tenets of the soft commitment HRM model, while the reality experienced by employees is more concerned with strategic control advocated by the hard HRM model. That the superficial implementation of high commitment management practices on the part of employer organizations could create employee frustration through falsely raised expectations and unfulfilled promises, clearly indicating the dominance of control over commitment values, cannot be denied. At the same time, it must be recognized that the problem may not lie with the practices per se but with their implementation, resulting in a situation where the rhetoric of commitment barely masks the underlying control philosophy (Houlihan, 2004). It appears, then, that the appropriate implementation of high commitment management practices coupled with a review of technobureaucratic controls may be a step in the right direction.

References

Abbott, A. 1988. *The System of the Professions: An Essay on the Division of Expert Labour*. Chicago: University of Chicago Press.
———. 1991. 'The Order of Professionalization: An Empirical Analysis', *Work and Occupations*, 18(4): 355–84.
Alvesson, M. 2001. 'Knowledge Work: Ambiguity, Image and Identity', *Human Relations*, 54(7): 863–78.
Alvesson, M. and D. Karreman. 2004. 'Interfaces of Control: Technocratic and Socio-ideological Control in a Global Management Consultancy Firm', *Accounting, Organizations and Society*, 29(3–4): 423–44.
Alvesson, M. and H. Willmott. 2002. 'Identity Regulation as Organizational Control: Producing the Appropriate Individual', *Journal of Management Studies*, 39(5): 619–44.
Ashforth, B.E. and R.H. Humphrey. 1993. 'Emotional Labour in Service Roles: The Influence of Identity', *Academy of Management Review*, 18(1): 88–115.
Baer, W. 1986. 'Expertise and Professional Standards', *Work and Occupations*, 13(4): 532–52.
Bain, P. and P. Taylor. 1999. 'Employee Relations, Worker Attitudes and Trade Union Representation in Call Centres', paper presented at the 17th Annual International Labour Process Conference, Royal Holloway College, University of London, 29–31 March.
———. 2000. 'Entrapped by the Electronic Panopticon?: Worker Resistance in the Call Centre', *New Technology, Work and Employment*, 15(1): 2–18.
———. 2001. 'Seizing the Time? Union Recruitment Potential in Scottish Call Centres', *Scottish Affairs*, 37(Autumn): 104–28.
———. 2002. 'Ringing the Changes: Trade Organization in Call Centres in the Financial Sector', *Industrial Relations Journal*, 33(3): 246–61.
Bain, P., P. Taylor, K. Gilbert and G. Gall. 2004. 'Failing to Organize or Organizing to Fail? Challenge, Opportunity and the Limitations of Union Policy in Four Call Centres', in W. Brown, G. Healy, E. Heery and P. Taylor (eds), *The Future of Worker Representation*, pp. 62–80. Basingstoke, UK: Palgrave Macmillan.
Bakker, A.B., E. Demerouti and W.B. Schaufeli. 2003. 'Dual Processes at Work in Call Centres: An Application of the Job Demands Resources Model', *European Journal of Work and Organizational Psychology*, 12(4): 393–417.
Banerjee, D. 2006. 'Information Technology, Productivity Growth, and Reduced Leisure: Revisiting the End of History', *Working USA: The Journal of Labour and Society*, 9(2): 199–213.
Batt, R. 2000. 'Strategic Segmentation in Front-line Services: Matching Customers, Employees and Human Resource Systems', *International Journal of Human Resource Management*, 11(3): 540–61.

Batt, R. 2001. 'Explaining Wage Inequality in Telecommunications Services: Customer Segmentation, Human Resource Practices and Union Decline', *Industrial and Labour Relations Review*, 54(2A): 425–59.

Batt, R. and L. Moynihan. 2002. 'The Viability of Alternative Call Centre Models', *Human Resource Management Journal*, 12(4): 14–34.

Batt, R., V. Doellgast and H. Kwon. 2005a. *The Indian Call Centre Industry: National Benchmarking Report*. Ithaca, NY: Cornell University.

———. 2005b. *Service Management and Employment Systems in U.S. and Indian Call Centres*. Ithaca, NY: Cornell University.

Belt, V., R. Richardson and J. Webster. 1999a. 'Smiling Down the Phone: Women's Work in Telephone Call Centres', Workshop on Call Centres, March 1999. London: London School of Economics.

———. 2000. 'Women's Work in the Information Economy', *Information Communication and Society*, 3(3): 366–85.

———. 2002. 'Women, Social Skill and Interactive Service Work in Telephone Call Centres', *New Technology, Work and Employment*, 17(1): 20–34.

Belt, V., R. Richardson, J. Webster, M. van Klaveren and K. Tidjens. 1999b. 'Work Opportunities for Women in the Information Society: Call Centre Teleworking (WOWIS)', Executive Summary of Final Report to the Information Society Project Office of the European Commission. Available online at http://www.campus.ncl.ac.uk/unbs/curds/pubsOL.asp (downloaded on 31 August 2008).

Benson, S. 1986. *Counter Cultures*. Chicago: University of Illinois Press.

Bishop, A. and J. Scudder. 1991. *Nursing: The Practice of Caring*. New York: National League for Nursing Press.

Bowen, D.E. and E.E. Lawler. 1992. 'The Empowerment of Service Workers: What, Why, How and When', *Sloan Management Review*, 33(3): 31–39.

Brændengen, T. 1999. 'Managerial Practices and Implications for the Shop-floor Culture: A Call Centre in the UK Insurance Industry', paper presented at the 17th International Labour Process Conference, Royal Holloway College, London, 29–31 March.

Brannan, M.J. 2005. 'Once More with Feeling: Ethnographic Reflections on the Mediation of Tension in a Small Team of Call Centre Workers', *Gender, Work and Organization*, 12(5): 420–39.

Bryman, A. 1988. *Quality and Quantity in Social Research*. London: Unwin Hyman.

Bryman, A. and R.G. Burgess. 1999. 'Qualitative Research Methodology: A Review', in A. Bryman and R.G. Burgess (eds), *Qualitative Research*, Volume I, pp. ix–xlvi. London: Sage Publications.

Buchanan, R.M. and S. Koch-Schulte. 2000. *Gender on the Line: Technology, Restructuring and the Reorganization of Work in the Call Centre Industry*. Ottawa: Status of Women Canada.

Budhwar, P., A. Varma, V. Singh and R. Dhar. 2006. 'HRM Systems of Indian Call Centres: An Exploratory Study', *International Journal of Human Resource Management*, 17(5): 881–97.

Burch, R. 1989. 'On Phenomenology and its Practices', *Phenomenology + Pedagogy*, 7: 187–217.

Burger, J.M. 2004. *Personality*. Belmont, CA: Wadsworth.

Call Centres. 2002. *Reward and Work-life Strategies*. London: Industrial Relations Services.
Callaghan, G. and P. Thompson. 2001. 'Edwards Revisited: Technical Control and Call Centres', *Economic and Industrial Democracy*, 22(1): 13–37.
Caplow, T. 1964. *The Sociology of Work*. New York: McGraw-Hill.
Cohen, L. and A. El-Sawad. 2007. 'Accounting for "us" and "them": Indian and UK Customer Service Workers' Reflections on Offshoring', *Economic and Political Weekly*, 42(21): 1951–57.
Cohen, L. and R.W. Hurd. 1998. 'Fear, Conflict, and Union Organizing', in K. Bronfenbrenner, S. Friedman, R.W. Hurd, R.A. Oswald (eds), *Organizing to Win: New Research on Union Strategies*, pp. 19–36. Ithaca, NY: Industrial and Labour Relations Press.
Cohen, M.Z. and A. Omery. 1994. 'Schools of Phenomenology: Implications for Research', in J.M. Morse (ed.), *Critical Issues in Qualitative Research Methods*, pp. 136–57. California: Sage Publications.
Cowie, C. 2007. 'The Accents of Outsourcing: The Meanings of Neutral in the Indian Call Centre Industry', *World Englishes*, 26(3): 316–30.
Creswell, J.W. 1998. *Qualitative Inquiry and Research Design: Choosing among Five Traditions*. California: Sage Publications.
Crompton, R. 1990. 'Professions in the Current Context', *Work, Employment and Society*, 4(5): 147–66.
D'Cruz, P. and E. Noronha. 2006. 'Being Professional: Organizational Control in Indian Call Centres', *Social Science and Computer Review*, 24(3): 342–61.
———. 2007. 'Technical Call Centres: Beyond Electronic Sweatshops and Assembly Lines in the Head', *Global Business Review*, 8(1): 53–67.
———. 2008. 'Doing Emotional Labour: The Experiences of Indian Call Centre Agents', *Global Business Review*, 9(1): 131–47.
DeCotiis, T. and J. Le Louarn. 1981. 'A Predictive Study of Voting Behaviour in a Representation Election Using Union Instrumentality and Work Perceptions', *Organization Behaviour and Human Performance*, 27(1): 103–18.
Deery, S., R. Iverson and J. Walsh. 2002. 'Work Relationships in Telephone Call Centres: Understanding Emotional Exhaustion and Employee Withdrawal', *Journal of Management Studies*, 39(4): 471–96.
———. 2004. 'The Effect of Customer Service Encounters on Job Satisfaction and Emotional Exhaustion', in S. Deery and N. Kinnie (eds), *Call Centres and Human Resource Management*, pp. 471–96. New York: Palgrave.
Deery, S. and N. Kinnie. 2004. 'Introduction: The Nature and Management of Call Centre Work', in S. Deery and N. Kinnie (eds), *Call Centres and Human Resource Management*, pp. 1–22. New York: Palgrave.
Deetz, S. 1995. *Transforming Communication, Transforming Business: Building Responsive and Responsible Workplaces*. Cresskill, NJ: Hampton Press.
Demerouti, E., A.B. Bakker, F. Nachreiner and W.B. Schaufeli. 2001. 'The Job Demands Resources Model of Burnout', *Journal of Applied Psychology*, 86(3): 499–512.
Denzin, N.K. and Y.S. Lincoln. 1994. 'Introduction: Entering the Field of Qualitative Research', in N.K. Denzin and Y.S. Lincoln (eds), *Handbook of Qualitative Research*, pp. 1–19. California: Sage Publications.

Devine, F., N.J. Britton, R. Mellor and P. Halfpenny. 2000. 'Professional Work and Professional Careers in Manchester's Business and Financial Sector', *Work, Employment and Society*, 14(3): 521–40.

Dietrich, M. and J. Roberts. 1999. 'Beyond the Economics of Professionalism', in J. Broadbent, M. Dietrich. and J. Roberts (eds), *The End of the Professions?: The Restructuring of Professional Work*, pp.14–33. Oxon, UK: Routledge.

Dormann, C. and F. Zijlstra. 2003. 'Call Centres: High on Technology, High on Emotions', *European Journal of Work and Organizational Psychology*, 12(4): 305–10.

Dossani, R. and M. Kenney. 2003. *Went for Cost, Stayed for Quality? Moving the Back Office to India*. Stanford, CA: Asia Pacific Research Centre, Stanford University.

Du Gay, P. and G. Salaman. 1992. 'The Cult(ure) of the Customer', *Journal of Management Studies*, 29(5): 615–33.

Erickson, R.J. and A.S. Wharton. 1997. 'Inauthenticity and Depression: Assessing the Consequences of Interactive Service Work', *Work and Occupations*, 24(2): 188–213.

Evetts, J. 2003. 'The Sociological Analysis of Professionalism: Occupational Change in the Modern World', *International Sociology*, 18(2): 395–415.

———. 2006. 'Short Note: The Sociology of Professional Groups: New Directions', *Current Sociology*, 54(1): 133–43.

Faia, M.A. 1976. 'Will Unions Make Us Less Professional?', *College English*, 38(1): 1–14.

Falk, W.F., M.D. Grimes and G.F. Lord, III. 1982. 'Professionalism and Conflict in a Bureaucratic Setting: The Case of a Teachers' Strike', *Social Problems*, 29(5): 551–59.

Farrell, N. 2006. 'Indian Call Centres are Both Sodom and Gomorrah: Take Archbishop of Bangalore Notions with a Pillar of Salt. Tuesday 14 November 2006'. Available online at http://www.theinquirer.net/default.aspx?article=35715 (downloaded on 28 August 2008).

Fernie, S. and D. Metcalfe. 1998. '(Not) Hanging on the Telephone: Payment Systems in the New Sweatshops.' London: Centre for Economic Performance, London School of Economics. Available online at cep.lse.ac.uk/pubs/download/dp0390.pdf (downloaded on 31 August 2008).

Financial Express. 2005. 'The IT–ITes Sector has the Best HR Practices', *Financial Times*, 31 October 2005. Available online at http://www.financialexpress.com/news/The-IT-ITeS-sector-has-the-best-HR-practices/155920/ (downloaded on 19 August 2008).

Fletcher, B. Jr. and R.W. Hurd. 1998. 'Beyond the Organizing Model: The Transformation Process in Local Unions', in K. Bronfenbrenner, S. Friedman, R.W. Hurd, R.A. Oswald (eds), *Organizing to Win: New Research on Union Strategies*, pp. 37–53. Ithaca, NY: Industrial and Labor Relations Press.

Forsyth, P. and T. Danisiewicz. 1985. 'Toward a Theory of Professionalization', *Work and Occupations*, 12(1): 59–76.

Fournier, V. 1999. 'The Appeal to "Professionalism" as a Disciplinary Mechanism', *The Sociological Review*, 47(2): 280–307.

Freidson, E. 1970. *Professional Dominance: The Social Structure of Medical Care*. New York: Atherton Press.

———. 1984. 'The Changing Nature of Professional Control', *Annual Reviews in Sociology*, 10: 1–20.

Freidson, E. 2001. *Professionalism: The Third Logic*. Britain: Blackwell.
Frenkel, S., M. Korczynski, K. Shire and M. Tam. 1998. 'Beyond Bureaucracy: Work Organization in Call Centres', *International Journal of Human Resource Management*, 9(6): 957–79.
———. 1999. *On the Frontline: Organization of Work in the Information Economy*. Ithaca, NY: Cornell University Press.
Fuller, L. and V. Smith. 1991. 'Consumers' Reports: Management by Customers in a Changing Economy', *Work, Employment and Society*, 5(1): 1–16.
Gabriel, Y. 1999. 'Beyond Happy Families: A Critical Reevaluation of the Control-Resistance-Identity Triangle', *Human Relations*, 52(2): 179–203.
Garson, B. 1988. *The Electronic Sweatshop: How Computers are Transforming the Office of the Future into the Factory of the Past*. New York: Simon & Schuster.
Glasner, H. 1979. 'Professional Power and State Intervention in Medical Practice', *Journal of Sociology*, 15(3): 20–29.
Grebner, S., N.K. Semmer, L.L. Faso, S. Gut, W. Kalin and A. Elfering. 2003. 'Working Conditions, Well-being and Job-related Attitudes among Call Centre Agents', *European Journal of Work and Organizational Psychology*, 12(4): 341–65.
Greenwood, E. 1962. 'Attributes of a Profession', in S. Nosow and W. H. Form (eds), *Man, Work, and Society*, pp. 206–18. New York: Basic Books.
Gutek, B. 1995. *The Dynamics of Service: Reflections on the Changing Nature of Customer/Provider Interactions*. San Francisco: Jossey-Bass.
Haines, L. 2006. 'Catholic Church Bemoans Call Centre Bacchanalia Indian "Dens of iniquity"'. Monday 9 October 2006. Available online at http://www.theregister.co.uk/2006/10/09/dens_of_iniquity/ (downloaded on 28 August 2008).
Hamilton, P.M. 2001. 'Rhetoric and Employment Relations', *British Journal of Industrial Relations*, 39(3): 433–51.
Harrison, M.I. 1994. 'Professional Control as Process: Beyond Structural Theories', *Human Relations*, 47(10): 1201–31.
Hatch, M.J. and A.L. Cunliffe. 2006. *Organization Theory: Modern, Symbolic and Postmodern Perspectives*. New York: Oxford University Press.
Heery, E., J. Kelly and J. Waddington. 2003. 'Union Revitalization in Britain', *European Journal of Industrial Relation*, 9(1): 79–97.
Henriksson, L. 2006. 'Understanding Professional Projects in Welfare Service Work: Revival of Old Professionalism?', *Gender, Work and Organization*, 13(2): 174–92.
Herzenberg, S., J. Alic and H. Wial. 1998. *New Rules for a New Economy: Employment and Opportunity in Postindustrial America*. Ithaca, NY: Cornell University Press.
Hirschfeld, K. 2003. 'IT Professionals' Forum in India'. Available online at http://www.union-network.org/uniibitsn.nsf/0b216cc03f4649f6c125710f0044be29/$FILE/India03-E.pdf (downloaded on 19 August 2008).
———. 2005. 'IT Professionals' Forum in India: Organization at a Crossroad', Report on a visit to IT Professionals' Forum, February 2005. Available online at http://www.uniglobalunion.org/UNIsite/Groups/PMS/publications/ITPFIndia-En.pdf (downloaded on 28 August 2008).
Hochschild, A.R. 1983. *The Managed Heart*. Berkeley: University of California Press.
Holman, D.J. 2003. 'Call Centres', in D.J. Holman, T.W. Wall, C.W. Glegg, P. Sparrow and A. Howard (eds), *The New Workplace: A Guide to the Human Impact of Modern Working Practices*, pp. 115–34. Chichester, UK: Wiley.

References

Holman, D.J. 2004. 'Employee Well-being in Call Centres', in S. Deery and N. Kinnie (eds), *Call Centres and Human Resource Management*, pp. 223–44. New York: Palgrave.

Houlihan, M. 2000. 'Eyes Wide Shut? Querying the Depth of Call Centre Learning', *Journal of European Industrial Training*, 24(2/4): 228–40.

———. 2001. 'Managing to Manage? Stories from the Call Centre Floor', *Journal of European Industrial Training*, 25(2/3/4): 208–20.

———. 2004. 'Tensions and Variations in Call Centre Management Strategies', in S. Deery and N. Kinnie (eds), *Call Centres and Human Resource Management*, pp. 57–101. New York: Palgrave.

Hughes, E. 1963. 'Professions', *Daedalus*, 92(Fall): 655–68.

Hurd, R.W. 2000. 'Professional Workers, Unions and Association: Affinities and Antipathies', background paper prepared for the Albert Shanker Institute Seminar on Unions Organizing Professionals, Summer 2000. Available online at http://www.ashankerinst.org/Downloads/hurd.doc (downloaded on 31 August 2008).

Hutchinson, S., J. Purcell and N. Kinnie. 2000. 'Evolving High Commitment Management: The Experience of the RAC Call Centre', *Human Resource Management*, 10(1): 63–78.

Hyman, J., C. Baldry, D. Scholarios and D. Bunzel. 2003. 'Work-life Imbalance in Call Centres and Software Development', *British Journal of Industrial Relations*, 41(2): 215–39.

Indiatimes. 2005. 'No Trade Union for Indian BPO Workers', *Indiatimes News Network*, Monday, 31 October 2005. Available online at http://infotech.indiatimes.com/BPO__ITES/Outsourcing/No_trade_union_for_Indian_BPO_workers/articleshow/1281025.cms (downloaded on 19 August 2008).

ITPF. 2007. 'Chairman's Message'. Available online at http://www.itpfindia.org/india/content/view/58/63/ (downloaded on 24 February 2007).

Iype, G. 2005. 'Does the IT Industry Need a Trade Union?', *Rediff News*, 6 October 2005. Available online at http://www.rediff.com/money/2005/oct/06bspec.htm (downloaded on 19 August 2008).

Jayanth, V. 2007. 'Any Slowdown in the IT Industry Can Have a Cascading Effect: Lakshmi Narayanan', *The Hindu*, 20 October 2007. Available online at http://www.hinduonnet.com/2007/10/20/stories/2007102056571300.htm (downloaded on 19 August 2008).

Jha, M.S. and M.B. Chatterjee. 2006. 'Call Centres to Hear From Unions Again', *Economic Times*, 3 October 2006. Available online at http://economictimes.indiatimes.com/articleshow/2069857.cms (downloaded on 19 August 2008).

Jessup, D.K. 1978. 'Teacher Unionization: A Reassessment of Rank and File Motivations', *Sociology of Education*, 51(1): 44–45.

Johnson, T. 1972. *Professions and Power*. London: Macmillan.

Khaleej Times Online. 2006. 'Sex Life of Call-centre Workers Fascinates India', Khaleej Times Online, 13 November 2006. Available online at http://www.khaleejtimes.com/DisplayArticle.asp?xfile=data/todaysfeatures/2006/November/todaysfeatures_November28.xml&section=todaysfeatures (downloaded on 28 August, 2008).

Khurana, R., N. Nohria and D. Prenrice. 2005. 'Is Business Management a Profession?', HBS Working Knowledge, Harvard Business School. Available online at http://hbswk.hbs.edu/item/4650.html (downloaded on 31 August 2008).

Kinnie, N., J. Purcell and S. Hutchinson. 1999. 'Modeling HR Practices and Business Strategy in Telephone Call Centres', Workshop on Call Centres, 19 March. London: Centre for Economic Performance, London School of Economics.

Kinnie, N., S. Hutchinson and J. Purcell. 2000. 'Fun and Surveillance: The Paradox of High Commitment Management in Call Centres', *International Journal of Human Resource Management*, 11(5): 967–85.

Klegon, D. 1978. 'The Sociology of Professions: An Emerging Perspective', *Sociology of Work and Occupation*, 5(3): 259–83.

Knights, D. and D. McCabe. 1998. 'What Happens When the Phone Goes Wild?: Staff, Stress and Spaces for Escape in a BPR Telephone Banking Work Regime', *Journal of Management Studies*, 35(2): 163–94.

Knights, D. and G. Morgan. 1991. 'Corporate Strategy, Organizations and Subjectivity: A Critique', *Organization Studies*, 12(2): 251–73.

Korczynski, M. 2001. 'The Contradictions of Service Work: Call Centre as Customer-Oriented Bureaucracy', in A. Sturdy, I. Grugulis and H. Willmott (eds), *Customer Service: Empowerment and Entrapment*, pp. 79–101. Basingstoke, UK: Palgrave.

———. 2002. 'Call Centre Consumption and the Enchanting Myth of Customer Sovereignty', in U. Holtgrewe, K. Christian and K.A. Shire (eds), *Re-Organizing Service Work: Call Centres in Germany and Britain*, pp. 163–82. Aldershot, UK: Ashgate.

———. 2003. 'Communities of Coping: Collective Emotional Labour in Service Work', *Organization*, 10(1): 55–79.

Korczynski, M., K. Shire, S. Frenkel and M. Tam. 2000. 'Service Work in Consumer Capitalism', *Work, Employment and Society*, 14(4): 669–87.

Kornhauser, W. 1962. *Scientists in Industry: Conflict and Accommodation*. Berkeley: University of California Press.

Langan, T. 1970. 'The Future of Phenomenology', in F.J. Smith (ed.), *Phenomenology in Perspective*, pp. 1–15. The Hague: Martinus Nijhoff.

Lankshear, G. and D. Mason. 2001. 'Within the Panopticon? Surveillance, Privacy and the Social Relations of Work in Two Call Centres', paper presented at the Work, Employment and Society Conference, Nottingham, UK, 11–13 September 2001.

Larson, M. 1977. *The Rise of Professionalism: A Sociological Analysis*. London: University of California Press.

Latham, S.R. 2002. 'Medical Professionalism: A Parsonian View', *The Mount Sinai Journal of Medicine*, 69(6): 363–69.

Legge, K. 2006. 'Human Resource Management', in S. Ackroyd, R. Batt, P. Thompson and P.S. Tolbert (eds), *Oxford Handbook of Work and Organization*, pp. 220–41. Oxford: Oxford University Press.

Leicht, K.T. and M.L. Fennell. 2001. *Professional Work: A Sociological Approach*. Oxford: Blackwell.

Leidner, R. 1996. 'Rethinking Questions of Control', in C. Macdonald and C. Sirianni (eds), *Working in the Service Economy*, pp. 29–49. Philadelphia: Temple University Press.

Lewig, K.A. and M.F. Dollard. 2003. 'Emotional Dissonance, Emotional Exhaustion and Job Satisfaction in Call Centres Workers', *European Journal of Work and Organizational Psychology*, 12(4): 366–92

References

Lincoln, Y. and E. Guba. 1985. *Naturalistic Inquiry*. California: Sage Publications.
———. 1999. 'Establishing Trustworthiness', in A. Bryman and R.G. Burgess (eds), *Qualitative Research*, Volume 3, pp. 397–444. California: Sage Publications.
Macdonald, C.L. and C. Sirianni. 1996. *Working in the Service Society*. Philadelphia: Temple University Press.
Macdonald, K. 1995. *The Sociology of Professions*. London: Sage Publications.
Marshall, T.H. 1962. 'Professionalism and Social Policy', in S. Nosow and W. Form (eds), *Man, Work and Society*, pp. 225–35. New York: Basic Books.
Mason, D., G. Button, G. Lankshear and S. Coates. 2002. 'Getting Real about Surveillance and Privacy at Work', in S. Woolgar (ed.), *Virtual Society? Technology Cyberbole, Reality*, pp. 99–114. Oxford: Oxford University Press.
McMillin, D. 2006. 'Outsourcing Identities: Call Centres and Cultural Transformation in India', *Economic and Political Weekly*, 41(3): 235–41.
McPhail, B. 2002. 'What is on the Line in Call Centre Studies?'. Available online at http://www.fis.utoronto.ca/research/iprp/publications/mcphail-cc.pdf (downloaded on 10 August 2005).
McReynolds, P., J. Altrocchi and C. House. 2000. 'Self-pluralism: Assessment and Relations to Adjustment, Life Changes and Age', *Journal of Personality*, 68(2): 347–81.
Mehta, A., A. Armenakis, N. Mehta and F. Irani. 2006. 'Challenges and Opportunities of Business Process Outsourcing in India', *Journal of Labour Research*, 27(3): 324–38.
Middlehurst, R. and T. Kennie. 1999. 'Leading Professionals', in J. Broadbent, M. Dietrich and J. Roberts (eds), *The End of the Professions?: The Restructuring of Professional Work*, pp. 50–60. Oxon, UK: Routledge.
Miles, M.S. and A.M. Huberman. 1994. *Qualitative Data Analysis: A Sourcebook of New Methods*. California: Sage Publications.
Milton, L.P. 2003. 'An Identity Perspective on the Propensity of High-tech Talent to Unionize', *Journal of Labour Research*, 24(1): 31–53.
Mirchandani, Kiran. 2003a. 'Gender Eclipsed? Work Relations in Transnational Call Centers', paper presented at the Administrative Sciences Association of Canada 2003 Conference, Halifax, Nova Scotia.
———. Unpublished paper. 'Making Americans: Transnational Call Centre Work in India', available online at http://merlin.mngt.waikato.ac.nz/ejrot/cmsconference/2003/proceedings/postcolonial/Mirchandani.pdf (downloaded on 31 August 2008).
———. 2004. 'Practices of Global Capital: Gaps, Cracks and Ironies in Transnational Call Centres in India', *Global Networks*, 4(4): 355–73.
Mitter, S., G. Fernandez and S. Varghese. 2004. 'On the Threshold of Informalization: Women Call Centers in India', in M. Carr (ed.), *Chains of Fortune: Linking Women Producers and Workers with Global Markets*, pp. 165–83. London: Commonwealth Secretariat.
Morris, J.A. and D.C. Feldman. 1996. 'The Dimensions, Antecedents and Consequences of Emotional Labour', *Academy of Management Review*, 21(4): 986–1010.

Morse, J.M. 1991. 'Qualitative Nursing Research: A Free-for-all?', in J.M. Morse (ed.), *Qualitative Nursing Research: A Contemporary Dialogue*, pp. 14–22. California: Sage Publications.

Mulholland, K. 1999. 'Back to the Future: A Call Centre and New Forms of Direct Control', paper presented at the 17th Annual International Labour Process Conference, 29–31 March 1999. School of Management, Royal Holloway, University of London.

———. 2002. 'Gender, Emotional Labour and Teamworking in a Call Centre', *Personnel Review*, 31(3): 283–303.

Nahar, S. 2006. 'India's Call Centre Staff Speak Out', *BBC News*, 14 December 2006. Available online at http://news.bbc.co.uk/2/hi/business/6162973.stm (downloaded on 19 August 2008).

Nanda, A. 2005. *Who is a Professional?*. Boston: Harvard Business School.

NASSCOM. not dated a. 'Tech Titans Tip on Farmland Debate—NASSCOM Wants Stake for Sons of Soil.' Available online at http://www.nasscom.in/Nasscom/templates/NormalPage.aspx?id=50648 (downloaded on 19 August 2008).

———. not dated b. 'National Skills Registry—Fact Sheet.' Available online at http://www.nasscom.in/upload/5216/Factsheet-NSR%20Aug%2023%202007.doc (downloaded on 28 August 2008).

———. not dated c. 'Indian Security Environment—Fact Sheet.' Available online at www.nasscom.in/upload/5216/Indian%20Security%20Environment%202005-06%20July%2006.pdf (downloaded on 28 August 2008).

———. not dated d. 'Data Security Council of India (DSCI): A Self-Regulatory Initiative in Data Security and Privacy Protection'. Available online at www.nasscom.in/upload/5216/Datasecurity.pdf (downloaded on 28 August 2008).

———. 2003. *Strategic Review 2003*. New Delhi: NASSCOM.

———. 2005a. *Strategic Review 2005*. New Delhi: NASSCOM.

———. 2005b. 'Executive Summary'. Available online at www.bpo.nasscom.org/artdisplay.aspx?cat_id=619 (downloaded on 19 August 2008).

———. 2006. *Strategic Review 2006*. New Delhi: NASSCOM.

———. 2007a. *India ITES–BPO Strategy Summit 2007: Background and Reference Source*. New Delhi: NASSCOM.

———. 2007b. *Strategic Review 2007*. New Delhi: NASSCOM.

NASSCOM–McKinsey. 2005. *Extending India's Leadership of the Global IT and BPO Industries*. New Delhi: NASSCOM–McKinsey.

Ng, C. and S. Mitter. 2005. 'Valuing Women's Voices: Call Centre Workers in Malaysia and India', *Gender, Technology and Development*, 9(2): 209–33.

Noon, M. and P. Blyton. 1997. *The Realities of Work*. Basingstoke, UK: Macmillan.

Noronha, E. 1996. 'Liberalization and Industrial Relations', *Economic and Political Weekly*, 31(8): L14–L21.

———. 2005. *Ethnicity in Industrial Organizations*. New Delhi: Rawat.

Noronha, E. and P. D'Cruz. 2006. 'Organizing Call Centre Agents: Emerging Issues', *Economic and Political Weekly*, 41(21): 2115–21.

———. 2007. 'Reconciling Dichotomous Demands: Telemarketing Agents in Bangalore and Mumbai, India', *The Qualitative Report*, 12(2): 255–80.

Noronha, E. and P. D'Cruz. *Global Sourcing and Remote Work: India Country Study*. Report prepared for ILO Geneva. Ahmedabad: IIM Ahmedabad.

———. 2008b. 'The Exit Coping Response to Workplace Bullying: HRM Paves the Way', paper presented at the 6th International Conference on Workplace Bullying, Montreal, Canada, 4–6 June.

Outsourcing Times. 2005. 'The Call Centers Association of India Opposes Left Call for Unionism.' Available online at http://www.blogsource.org/2005/10/the_call_center.html (downloaded on 24 February 2007).

Patel, R. 2006. 'Working the Night Shift: Gender and the Global Economy', *ACME: An International E-Journal for Critical Geographies*, 5(1): 9–27.

Patton, M.Q. 1990. *Qualitative Evaluation and Research Methods*. California: Sage Publications.

Paul, J. and U. Huws. 2002. *How Can We Help? Good Practice in Call Centre Employment*. Brussels: European Trade Union Confederation.

Pavalko, R.M. 1971. *Sociology of Occupations and Professions*. Itasca, IL: FE Peacock.

Poster, W. 2007. 'Who's on the Line? Indian Call Centre Agents Pose as Americans for US Outsourced Firms', *Industrial Relations*, 46(2): 271–304.

Purcell, J. and N. Kinnie. 2000. 'Employment Regimes for the Factories of the Future: Human Resource Management in Telephone Call Centres', paper presented at the National Academy of Management Symposium on 'Employment Relationship, Culture and Work Modes within the Strategic Human Resource Architecture', Toronto, Canada, 4–9 August.

Rabban, D.M. 1991. 'Is Unionization Compatible with Professionalism?', *Industrial and Labour Relations Review*, 45(1): 97–112.

Raelin, J.A. 1989. 'Unionization and Deprofessionalization: Which Comes First?', *Journal of Organizational Behaviour*, 10(2): 101–15.

Ramaswamy, E.A. 1985. 'Managerial Trade Unions', *Economic and Political Weekly*, 20(21): M 75–88.

———. 1997. *A Question of Balance: Labour, Management and Society*. Delhi: Oxford University Press.

Ramesh, B. 2004. 'Cybercoolies in BPOs', *Economic and Political Weekly*, 39(5): 492–97.

Ray, M.A. 1994. 'The Richness of Phenomenology: Philosophic, Theoretic, and Methodologic Concerns', in J. M. Morse (ed.), *Critical Issues in Qualitative Research Methods*, pp. 117–33. California: Sage Publications.

Richardson, R., V. Belt and N. Marshall. 2000. 'Taking Calls to Newcastle: The Regional Implications of the Growth in Call Centres', *Regional Studies*, 34(4): 357–69.

Richardson, R. and J.N. Marshall. 1999. 'Teleservices, Call Centres and Urban and Regional Development', *Service Industries Journal*, 19(1): 96–116.

Rose, E. and G. Wright. 2005. 'Satisfaction and Dimensions of Control among Call Centre Customer Service Representatives', *International Journal of Human Resource Management*, 16(1): 136–60

Rousseau, D.M. 1990. 'New Hire Perceptions of Their Own and Their Employer's Obligations: A Study of Psychological Contracts', *Journal of Organizational Behaviour*, 11(5): 389–400.

Schwandt, T.A. 1997. *Qualitative Inquiry: A Dictionary of Terms*. California: Sage Publications.

Sciulli, D. 2005. 'Continental Sociology of Professions Today: Conceptual Contributions', *Current Sociology*, 53(6): 915–42.

Seidman, J. and G.G. Cain. 1964. 'Unionized Engineers and Chemists: A Case Study of a Professional Union', *Journal of Business*, 37(3): 238–57.

Sheth, N.R. 1993. 'Our Trade Unions: An Overview', *Economic and Political Weekly*, 28(6): 231–36.

———. 1996. 'We, the Trade Unions', *Indian Journal of Industrial Relations*, 32(1): 1–17.

Shire, K., U. Holtgrewe and C. Kerst. 2002. 'Re-organizing Customer Service Work: An Introduction', in U. Holtgrewe, K. Christian and K.A. Shire (eds), *Re-organizing Service Work: Call Centres in Germany and Britain*, pp. 1–16. Aldershot, UK: Ashgate.

Singh, P. and A. Pandey. 2005. 'Women in Call Centres', *Economic and Political Weekly*, 40(7): 684–88.

Sisson, K. 1994. 'Personnel Management: Paradigms, Practices and Prospects', in K. Sisson (ed.), *Personnel Management: A Comprehensive Guide to Theory and Practice*, pp. 3–50. Oxford: Blackwell.

Snider, H.W. 1963. 'Problems of Professionalism', *Journal of Insurance*, 30(4): 563–72.

Spicer, A and P. Fleming. 2004. 'You can Checkout Anytime, But You can Never Leave: Spatial Boundaries in a High Commitment Organization', *Human Relations*, 57(1): 75–94.

Spiegelberg, H. 1982. *The Phenomenologic Movement: A Historical Introduction*. The Hague: Martinus Nijhoff.

Srinivasan, N. 1989. 'Growth of Professional Managerial Unionism: The Indian Experience', *Economic and Political Weekly*, 25(47): M-169–74.

Stanworth, C. 1997. 'Telework and the Information Age', *New Technology, Work and Employment*, 13(1): 51–62.

Storey, J. 1993. 'The Take-up of Human Resource Management by Mainstream Companies', *International Journal of Human Resource Management*, 4(3): 529–53.

———. 2001. *Human Resource Management: A Critical Text*. London: Thomson Learning.

Strauss, A. and J. Corbin. 1998. *Basics of Qualitative Research*. California: Sage Publications.

Strauss, G. 1964. 'Professional or Employee-Oriented: Dilemma for Engineering Unions', *Industrial and Labour Relations Review*, 17(4): 519–33.

Sturdy, A. and S. Fineman. 2001. 'Struggles for the Control of Affect: Resistance as Politics and Emotion', in A. Sturdy, A. Gruglis and H. Willmott (eds), *Customer Service, Empowerment and Entrapment*, pp. 135–56. London: Palgrave.

Taylor, P. and P. Bain. 1999. 'An Assembly Line in the Head: Work and Employment Relations in the Call Centre', *Industrial Relations Journal*, 30(2): 101–17.

———. 2001. 'Trade Unions, Workers' Rights and the Frontier of Control in UK Call Centres', *Economic and Industrial Democracy*, 22(1): 39–66.

———. 2003a. 'Subterranean Worksick Blues: Humour as Subversion in Two Call Centres', *Organization Studies*, 24(9): 1487–509.

———. 2003b. *Call Centres in Scotland and Outsourced Competition from India*. Glasgow and Stirling Universities: Scotecon.

Taylor, P. and P. Bain. 2003c. 'Call Centre Organizing in Adversity: From Excell to Vertex', in Gregor Gall (ed.), *Union Organizing: Campaigning for Union Recognition*, pp. 153–72. London: Routledge.

———. 2005. 'India Calling to the Faraway Towns: The Call Centre Labour Process and Globalization', *Work, Employment and Society*, 19(2): 261–82.

———. 2006. *An Investigation into the Offshoring of Financial Services Business Processes*. Glasgow, UK: University of Strathclyde.

———. 2008. 'United by a Common Language? Trade Union Responses in the UK and India to Call Centre Offshoring', *Antipode*, 40(1): 131–54.

Taylor, P., C. Baldry, P. Bain and V. Ellis. 2003. 'A Unique Working Environment: Health, Sickness and Absence Management in UK Call Centres', *Work, Employment and Society*, 17(3): 435–58.

Taylor, P., D. Scholarios, E. Noronha and P. D'Cruz. 2007. *Employee Voice and Collective Formation in the Indian ITES–BPO Industry*. Bangalore: UNITES.

Taylor, P., E. Noronha, D. Scholarios and P. D'Cruz. 2008. 'Employee Voice and Collective Formation in the Indian ITES–BPO Industry', *Economic and Political Weekly*, 43(22): 37–46.

The Sydney Morning Herald. 2006. 'Call Centre Girls Have More Fun, but It's Blamed for Rise of New Delhi Belly', *The Sydney Morning Herald*, 11 October 2006. Available online at http://www.smh.com.au/news/world/call-centre-girls-have-more-fun/2006/10/10/1160246130071.html (downloaded on 28 August 2008).

The Telegraph. 2006. 'Who Says BPOs Don't Have Unions?', *The Telegraph*, Sunday, 5 November 2006. Available online at http://www.telegraphindia.com/1061105/asp/look/story_6950153.asp (downloaded on 19 August 2008).

Thompson, C. 1999. 'If You Could Just Provide Me with a Sample: Examining Sampling in Qualitative and Quantitative Research Papers', *Evidence Based Nursing*, 2(3): 68–70. Available online at http://ebn.bmjjournals.com/cgi/content/full/2/3/68 (downloaded on 20 October 2005).

Thompson, P., C. Warhurst and G. Callaghan. 2001. 'Ignorant Theory and Knowledge Workers', *Journal of Management Studies*, 38(7): 923–42.

Tisza, S. 2005. 'CWA Visit To India. 31 January–8 February 2005', Report by Steve Tisza, President CWA Local 4250, 806 North Dearborn Street, Chicago, Illinois 60610. Available online at http://www.cwalocal4250.org/outsourcing/binarydata/India%20Report.pdf (downloaded on 19 August 2008).

Todd, P., J. Eveline, L. Still and J. Skene. 2003. 'Management Responses to Unions in Australian Call Centres: Exclude, Tolerate or Embrace?', *Australian Bulletin of Labour*, 29(2): 162–76.

Toren, N. 1975. 'Deprofessionalization and its Sources', *Sociology of Work and Occupations*, 2(4): 323–37.

Townsend, K. 2005. 'Electronic Surveillance and Cohesive Teams: Room for Resistance in an Australian Call Centre?', *New Technology, Work and Employment*, 20(1): 47–59.

UNI. 2002. 'Organizing IT Professionals in India: An Organizing Model for High Tech Clusters Elsewhere.' Available online at http://www.union-network.org/uniibitsn.nsf/8af8fa565fa0cfbfc12570b600521298/f5c45db92f38470ec1256bdf00293670?OpenDocument (downloaded on 19 August 2008).

UNI. 2008. 'New Ideas to Reach Young Professionals'. Available online at http://www.apesma.asn.au/newsviews/misc/media/2008/new_ideas_reach_young_profs_27_03_08.pdf (downloaded on 19 August 2008).

UNI–APRO. 2005. 'Introducing UNI Apro's CBPOP Project.' Available online at http://www.union-network.org/UNIAPRON.nsf/aa46e8f772bb0978c1256f6d004157/0978058ebdc9a485c1257035003fb65c/$FILE12.%20Introducing%20UNI%20Apro's%20CBPOP%20Project,%2025%20June%202005.doc (downloaded on 6 May 2008).

van den Broek, D. 2003. 'Recruitment Strategies and Union Exclusion', *Relations Industrielles/Industrial Relations*, 58(3): 515–36.

———. 2004. 'We Have the Values: Customers, Control and Corporate Ideology in Call Centre Operations', *New Technology, Work and Employment*, 19(1): 2–12.

van Maanen, J. and G. Kunda. 1989. 'Real Feelings: Emotional Expression and Organizational Culture', in L.L. Cummings and B.M. Staw (eds), *Research in Organizational Behaviour*, Volume 11, pp. 43–104. Greenwich, CT: JAI Press.

van Manen, M. 1998. *Researching Lived Experience*. Canada: Althouse.

Watson, T.J. 1995. 'In Search of HRM: Beyond the Rhetoric and Reality Distinction or the Dog that Didn't Bark', *Personnel Review*, 24(4): 6–16.

———. 2003. 'Towards a Grown-up and Critical Academic HRM and the Need to Grow Out of Infantile "Hard and Soft HRM", "Rhetoric and Reality" and Functionalist Habits to Engage Critically with the Adult World of Employment Management', paper presented at the 3rd International Critical Management Studies Conference, Lancaster University, UK, 7–9 July.

Wharton, A.S. 1993. 'The Affective Consequences of Service Work: Managing Emotions on the Job, *Work and Occupations*, 20(2): 205–32.

Wilensky, H. 1964. 'The Professionalization of Everyone?', *American Journal of Sociology*, 70(2): 137–58.

Willmott, H.C. 1993. 'Strength is Ignorance; Slavery is Freedom: Managing Culture in Modern Organizations', *Journal of Management Studies*, 30(4): 515–52.

Zapf, D., A. Isic, M. Bechtoldt and P. Blau. 2003. 'What is Typical for Call Centre Jobs? Job Characteristics and Service Interactions in Different Call Centres', *European Journal of Work and Organizational Psychology*, 12(4): 311–40.

Zapf, D., C. Vogt, C. Seifert, H. Mertini and A. Isic. 1999. 'Emotion Work as a Source of Stress', *European Journal of Work and Organizational Psychology*, 8(3): 371–400.

Index

abusive customers, 91–94
academic debate, on professionalism, 131–44
   conceptual issues, 132–38
   Indian call centre agents, taxonomic and power approaches, 138–44
ACD system. *See* automatic call distribution (ACD) system
APESMA. *See* Association of Professional Engineers, Scientists and Managers, Australia (APESMA)
Aptech, 129
association, 121
Association of Professional Engineers, Scientists and Managers, Australia (APESMA), 114–15, 124
automatic call distribution (ACD) system, 11, 12, 78, 79

banking, financial services and insurance (BFSI), 42
Bank of Baroda, 119
BelAir, 128
BFSI. *See* banking, financial services and insurance (BFSI)
Bharat Sanchar Nigam Limited (BSNL), 119
blue-collar officers, 118
BM–Daksh, 40
BSNL. *See* Bharat Sanchar Nigam Limited (BSNL)

call centre agents, 3, 21
   ACD system to monitor, 79
   designations of, 101–02
   dressing of, 82–83
   emotional exhaustion in, 22
   impact of customers reaction on, 91
   influence of notion of professionalism on attitude, 91
   lifestyle and public image, 142–44
   professional judgement, 140–41
   responses to abusive customers, 91–94
   targets for inbound, 76
   taxonomic and power approaches to understand Indian, 138–44
   See also employees
call centre employees *vs.* IT professionals, 117
call centres
   defined, 1
   development, 1–2
   employee experiences of working in, 2
   professional approach adopted by, 105
   types of, 3
   working in Indian, 47–58
      cultural dimensions, 54–55
      gender issues, 55–56
      managerial concerns, 56–58
      personal and social life, 51–52
      recruitment and training, 48–49
      remuneration and working conditions, 52–54
      work systems and job design, 49–51
   work requirements in, 4–20
      centrality of emotional labour, 8–11
      employee resistance, 16–20
      employee skills, 5–8
      monitoring, surveillance and control, 11–16
      work systems and job design, 3–5
   See also India's ITES–BPO sector

call centre unionization, 162–64
career growth, 146–50
CBPOP. *See* Centre for BPO Professionals (CBPOP)
centrality of emotional labour, 8–11
Centre for BPO Professionals (CBPOP), 64, 115–16
　challenges faced by, 116–21
　registration of trade union by, 121
CIS. *See* customer interaction services (CIS)
COBIT. *See* Control Objectives for Information and related Technology (COBIT)
collective resistance, 19
computer telephony integration (CTI) software, 11, 12
conscientization, of agents, 112
Control Objectives for Information and related Technology (COBIT), 36
Convergys, 40
COPC. *See* Customer Operations Performance Centre (COPC)
cost-to-company (CTC), 155
CSR. *See* customer service representatives (CSR)
CTC. *See* cost-to-company (CTC)
CTI. *See* computer telephony integration (CTI) software
cultural dimensions, in Indian call centres, 54–55
cultural training, 85–86
culture management, 28
customer, primacy of, 83–94
　communication with customers, 83–85
　cultural training, 85–86
　linguistic training, 86–87
　locational masking, 87–90
　pseudonyms, 88–90
customer communication, 83–85, 91
customer interaction, emotional labour and, 9–10
customer interaction services (CIS), 41
Customer Operations Performance Centre (COPC), 35–36

customer reactions, 90–91
customer service representatives (CSR), 1, 19, 25

data analysis, 68–71
data collection, India's ITES–BPO sector, 64–66
Data Security Council of India, 142
Domestic Tariff Area (DTA), 37
dressing, 82–83
DTA. *See* Domestic Tariff Area (DTA)
Dutch phenomenology, 62

EHTP. *See* Electronic Hardware Technology Park (EHTP)
Electronic Hardware Technology Park (EHTP), 37
emotional exhaustion, 10
　in call centre agents, 22
　impact on employee, 23
emotional labour
　centrality of, 8–11
　and customer interaction, 9–10
　primacy of customer, 83–85
employee resistance, 16–20
　collective, 19
　hints of, 108–10
　team working and, 20
　against totalizing systems of surveillance and control, 18
　unemployment and, 18
employees
　control, 11–16
　emotional exhaustion impact on, 23
　experiences of working in call centres, 2
　impact of work on, 20–32
　　stress, 21–25
　　well-being of, 25–32
　monitoring and surveillance of, 11–16
　skills, 5–8
　well-being, 25–32
　See also call centre agents
employer organizations, facilities in, 100–101

Index

employment levels, in India's ITES–BPO, 43
employment patterns, in India's ITES–BPO sector, 43–47
EXL, 40
Export Oriented Units (EOU), 37
export revenues, of India's ITES–BPO, 34

F&A. *See* finance and accounting (F&A)
FDI. *See* foreign direct investment (FDI)
feedback, 82
FIET. *See* International Federation of Commercial, Clerical, Professional and Technical Employees (FIET)
finance and accounting (F&A) services, 41
foreign direct investment (FDI), 37

GE, 40
gender issues, in Indian call centres, 55–56
globalization, Indian ITES–BPO export and, 34–35

health-related problems, 23–24, 97
hermeneutic phenomenology, 62
Honeywell, 40
HR administration services, 41
HSBC, 39, 40
Human Resource (HR) practices, 15, 32
research on, 26–27

IBM, 39
ICT. *See* information and communication technology (ICT)
identity issues, resolving, 121–25
IJP. *See* internal job postings (IJP)
inbound call centres, 3
Indian call centre agents, taxonomic and power approaches to understand, 138–44
Indian third party call centres, 48, 68, 102
India's ITES–BPO sector, 34–47
data collection from, 64–66

employment levels, 43
employment patterns, 43–47
NASSCOM's role in, 34–47
nature of work, 41–43
number of employees in 2004–05, 114
organizational structure, 38–41
overview, 34–38
principal location for, 40
See also call centres
individualism and professionalism, 118
Industrial Disputes Act, 1947, 45, 124
information and communication technology (ICT), 1, 2, 114
management ideology and, 13
to monitor workers, 12–13
information Technology Enabled Services–Business Process Outsourcing (ITES–BPO) sector. *See* ITES–BPO sector
Infosys, 39, 40
interactive voice response (IVR) technology, 12
internal job postings (IJP), 103
International Federation of Commercial, Clerical, Professional and Technical Employees (FIET), 112
International Standards Organization (ISO), 35
ITES–BPO employees, 117
collectivization, 121
under Industrial Disputes Act, 124
professional orientation, 123
resolving identity issues, 121–25
stand towards unions, 120–21
trade unions support to, 119
ITES–BPO sector, 2
collectivise in, 112–16
India's, 34–47
employment patterns, 43–47
nature of work, 41–43
organizational structure, 38–41
overview, 34–38
ITPF. *See* IT Professionals' Forum (ITPF)

IT Professionals' Forum (ITPF), 64, 112–16
   anti-union position leaders in, 115–16
   educational opportunities provided by, 114–15
   formation of, 112–13
IT professionals *vs.* call centre employees, 117
IT Services Management (ITSM), 36
ITSM. *See* IT Services Management (ITSM)
IVR. *See* interactive voice response (IVR) technology

JDR model. *See* job demands resources (JDR) model
job demands resources (JDR) model, 30
job design, 3–5
   in Indian call centres, 49–51
   technobureaucratic controls and, 81
job satisfaction
   emotional exhaustion and, 10
   intrinsic and extrinsic, 26
   job control and, 25, 26

knowledge process outsourcing (KPO), 42–43
KPO. *See* knowledge process outsourcing (KPO)
Krishna Group, 40

linguistic training, 86–87
locational masking, 87–90

managerial concerns, in Indian call centres, 56–58
managerial insights, in professionalism, 144–56
   career growth, 146–50
   informality and non-hierarchical structures, 145–46
   transparency in employer organizations functioning, 154–56
   workplace ambience, 150–54
Marxist analysis, of professions, 135

mass service/engineering model, 3–5
MNC captives, 40, 48, 66, 70
MNC third party, 48, 68, 70, 102
monitoring and surveillance, of emplyees, 11–16
mother tongue influence (MTI), 86
MphasiS, 40
MTI. *See* mother tongue influence (MTI)

NAC initiative. *See* NASSCOM's Assessment of Competence (NAC) initiative
NASSCOM. *See* National Association of Software and Service Companies (NASSCOM)
NASSCOM's Assessment of Competence (NAC) initiative, 139
National Association of Software and Service Companies (NASSCOM), 34–47, 141–42
National Skill Registry (NSR), 141
neo-Weberian perspective, of professions, 135
night shifts, working in, 94, 96
NIIT, 129
NSR. *See* National Skill Registry (NSR)

occupation. *See* profession
organizational control, 158
organizational requirements, 73–83
   adherence to job and organizational demands, 75–76
   punishments on failure to meet organizational expectations, 74
   restriction to carry anything, 78
   SLA, 73–74
   work in shifts, 73–74
   participants' adherence to, 75–76
organizational structure, in India's ITES–BPO sector, 38–41
outbound call centres, 3

participants, from Mumbai and Bangalore, 66–68
   data of, 67

Index

PD systems. *See* predictive dialling (PD) systems
personal life, in Indian call centres, 51–52
phenomenology, 60
predictive dialling (PD) systems, 11, 12
profession
    autonomy and, 139–40
    defined, 132
    Marxist analysis, 135
    power approaches to understand, 135–37
    structural–functional view of, 133–34
    taxonomic approaches to understand, 132–35
    trait model of, 132–33
professional autonomy, 132–33
professional identity, 73, 157–58
    collectivization and, 161–62
    cultivating agents, 108, 165–66
    cultivation of, 158
    gains from job and, 101–02
    ITES–BPO employees, 120
professionalism
    academic debate on, 131–44
    conceptual issues, 132–38
    Indian call centre agents, taxonomic and power approaches, 138–44
    adherence to job and organizational demands and, 75–76
    defined, 82
    identity regulation and, 158–59
    and individualism, 118
    influence on agents attitudes, 106–07
    managerial insights in, 144–56
    career growth, 146–50
    informality and non-hierarchical structures, 145–46
    transparency in employer organizations functioning, 154–56
    workplace ambience, 150–54
    privileges of, 100–108
professionalization, 132, 136–37

professional organization, 137
professionals
    defined, 132
    Parsons' view on, 133
Progeon, 40
pseudonyms, 88–90
pure plays, 39

qualitative research, 59–71
    data analysis, 68–71
    data collection, 64–66
    dimensions for comparing five research traditions in, 61
    methods, 63–64
    research strategy, 60–63
    study participants, 66–68
quality management team, 81

recruitment, in Indian call centres, 48–49
remuneration, in Indian call centres, 52–54
repetitive strain injury (RSI), 95
Reserve Bank of India (RBI), 37
RSI. *See* repetitive strain injury (RSI)

Satyam, 40
SEI CMM. *See* Software Engineering Institute Capability Maturity Model (SEI CMM)
sensitivity requirements, 9
service level agreement (SLA), 73–74, 80, 153, 155
Shops and Commercial Establishments Act, 44, 45
SIF. *See* Swedish Union for Technical and Clerical Employees (SIF)
skill development, 7
skills requirement, 5–8
SLA. *See* service level agreement (SLA)
small and medium enterprises (SME), 128
SME. *See* small and medium enterprises (SME)
social life, in Indian call centres, 51–52
social stressors, 29
Software Engineering Institute Capability Maturity Model (SEI CMM), 35

Software Technology Parks (STP), 37
Special Economic Zones (SEZ), 37
State Bank of India, 119
stress, 21–25
  coexistence with well-being, 28–29
structural–functional view, of professions, 133–34
Swedish Union for Technical and Clerical Employees (SIF), 113

task-related demands, 73–83
  adherence to, 75–76
task-related stress, 29
TCS, 40
team leader support
  research on, 26–27
team working, 20
technobureaucratic controls, 11–16, 73–83
  and job design, 81
technology dominated participants' work context, 78
thematic analysis, 68–71
Total Quality Management (TQM), 35
TQM. *See* Total Quality Management (TQM)
Trade Union Act, 124
training, in Indian call centres, 48–49
transparency, in organizations functioning, 154–56

UNI. *See* Union Network International (UNI)
Union for ITES (UNITES) Professionals, 64, 112, 125
  emphasis on social dialogue by, 126
  partnering employers, 125–27
  reconciling servicing and organizing, 127–30

Union Network International–Asia Pacific Regional Office (UNI–APRO), 69, 115
Union Network International (UNI), 112, 113
UNITES Professionals. *See* Union for ITES (UNITES) Professionals

verstehen, 69

WashTech, 113
well-being, employees, 25–32
  coexistence with, 28–29
Wipro, 39, 40
WNS, 40
working, in Indian call centres, 47–58
  cultural dimensions, 54–55
  gender issues, 55–56
  managerial concerns, 56–58
  personal and social life, 51–52
  recruitment and training, 48–49
  remuneration and working conditions, 52–54
  work systems and job design, 49–51
working conditions, in Indian call centres, 52–54
working in night shifts, 94, 96
workplace ambience, 150–54
work-related strain, 94–100
work requirements, in call centres
  centrality of emotional labour, 8–11
  employee resistance, 16–20
  employee skills, 5–8
  monitoring, surveillance and control, 11–16
work systems and job design, 3–5
work systems, 3–5
  in Indian call centres, 49–51

About the Authors

Ernesto Noronha is Associate Professor of Organizational Behaviour (OB) at the Indian Institute of Management (IIM) Ahmedabad, where he teaches Macro OB and Research Methodology. Dr Noronha's research interests include diversity at work, industrial relations, organizational change, organizational control, and ICTs and organizations. A PhD in Social Sciences from the Tata Institute of Social Sciences, Mumbai, Dr Noronha has held faculty positions at XLRI (Xavier Labour Relations Institute) Jamshedpur, IIT (Indian Institute of Technology) Kanpur and IIM (Indian Institute of Management) Kozhikode. He has previously published *Ethnicity in Industrial Organisations* (2005), apart from several international academic papers and presentations.

Premilla D'Cruz is Associate Professor of OB at IIM Ahmedabad. A PhD in Social Sciences from the Tata Institute of Social Sciences, Mumbai, Dr D'Cruz's research areas are emotions in organizations, self and identity, organizational control, and ICTs and organizations. She has published *Thinking Creatively at Work: A Sourcebook* (2008), *Family Care in HIV/AIDS: Exploring Lived Experience* (2004) and *In Sickness and in Health: The Family Experience of HIV/AIDS in India* (2003), in addition to numerous international papers and presentations. Dr D'Cruz has earlier held faculty appointments at IIT Kanpur and IIM Kozhikode. At IIM Ahmedabad, she teaches Micro OB and Creativity.